# PSYCHIC FAMILIES

Cassandra Eason

# PSYCHIC FAMILIES

## foulsham
LONDON • NEW YORK • TORONTO • SYDNEY

# foulsham

The Publishing House, Bennetts Close
Cippenham, Berks SL1 5AP, England

ISBN 0-572-02182-8

Copyright © 1995 Cassandra Eason

Typeset in Great Britain by Typesetting Solutions, Slough, Berks.
Printed in Great Britain by St. Edmundsbury Press, Bury St. Edmunds, Suffolk.

# CONTENTS

By the same author:

*Psychic Suburbia*
*Psychic Power of Children*
*Rune Divination for Today's Woman*
*Tarot Divination for Today's Woman*
*I Ching Divination for Today's Woman*
*Crystal Divination for Today's Woman*
*Moon Divination for Today's Woman*
*Pendulum Divination for Today's Woman*

# INTRODUCTION

I discovered the existence of the psychic family while I was researching the first version of my book, *The Psychic Power of Children*. Many childhood experiences led to recollections of similar events in the lives of mothers who were being interviewed about their children's magical insights. They would then go on to talk about their own mothers, and sometimes fathers, who were psychic, and occasionally could recall stories from family history about even earlier generations.

I was disturbed that the psychologists and psychiatrists with whom I discussed psychic families felt that the psychic family was a destructive unit. I assessed my own childhood and realised that I, too, had been part of a psychic unit. My mother and I had shared psychic secrets that had roots in her own childhood. She continued to haunt me after her death, but I closed my mind to psychic phenomena.

As a result I did not acknowledge my first two children's psychic experiences. Even when my middle son Jack had a dramatic telepathic link with his father that prompted my interest in the subject – he told me his dad was falling off his motorbike at the moment it was happening 40 miles away – I still regarded paranormal happenings in isolation. However, my younger three children have enjoyed a rich psychic world that has helped me to see that the psychic is a normal and healthy part of family life, and my change of attitude has enriched the lives of my two older children.

This book tells the stories of families who have encountered a world beyond the immediate. Surnames, and in some cases the area in which people live, have been omitted, to protect the identities of those whose stories are intensely personal. It is not a scientific study for you cannot take human experience and emotion into a laboratory and measure it. No one can repeat the emotion a mother feels when her child is in danger. No gauges or carefully calculated questionnaires can estimate the joy when an elderly person is reassured by a long-dead spouse, or met by a mother or brother as he or she faces 'the final mystery'.

We cannot easily dismiss as mere imagination those moments when people face birth, death or intense loneliness, and finding no worldly help, seem to reach beyond this world that is failing them, to loving hands waiting to help. Equally precious are those moments when a child reads our thoughts or a partner finishes a sentence prompted by some obscure train of thought that could not be anticipated on a conscious level.

If you read this book and can't accept the accounts of ordinary men and women as valid, then at least you have had an insight into the way many people do live, but perhaps never liked to mention. Ask your mum or gran about strange stories in your family or inexplicable remarks you made in your childhood. The few people I meet who cannot understand how people can believe such experiences and yet claim to be sane, usually say they have had a life totally untouched by sorrow and maybe deep love.

I have set out to show that intuitive links and shared psychic experiences should be welcomed, whether a telepathic link between parent and child or partners, a premonition of danger that if heeded can save someone we love, or grannies and grandads coming back to peep into the cot of a new arrival, or comfort a sick grandchild.

Over the past five years I have collected many stories of family psychic experiences, from both sides of the Atlantic and Australia, and have come to see that the bond of love can overcome the limits of time and space. For the family a psychic link is primarily one of love and is an assurance that we are not alone. It is for me perhaps the most exciting discovery that the psychic world is not one of weird seances or joyless experiments in university laboratories. In the following pages I hope to show that it touches the lives of many people as they laugh, cry and quarrel within that most annoying yet precious creation, the family.

As you read I hope you will write down your experiences to share with family members, and if you have time send them to me, through my publisher, so that, as with the other books I have written, the readers of one create the next.

Cassandra Eason, 1995

# 1

# THE PSYCHIC FAMILY

The family forms a natural psychic unit. When a child has a psychic experience, Mum, Grandma and less frequently, Dad, often recall psychic incidents in their own lives and family history. Some families have many such experiences across the generations.

Jennifer Moss is best known for her former role as Lucille Hewitt in the soap opera *Coronation Street*; she was the first and most famous child star of the Street. I met her on the set of Wire TV and she told me that, like many theatre people, she has a long psychic tradition, and a Spanish Romany grandfather:

'My mother was given a beautiful crystal ball that belonged to the family. As a child my grandfather would talk of his Romany mother. He told me that when someone died the caravan and all that person's possessions would be burned to set the spirit free.

'The first experience concerning my own life happened before my conception but was linked, as I found out later, with my gypsy ancestors. My parents had been trying for a child for 13 years and my mother had many operations to make her fertile. She decided in January 1944 to have one more operation and, if it failed, to accept that she might be childless.

'When my mother woke from the anaesthetic, an old nurse was standing over her. This was not surprising since in wartime many retired people returned to work. My mother asked the old nurse for a drink of water and they chatted. Then my mother, feeling drowsy, fell asleep after asking for a second drink. When she woke three or four hours later, the old nurse was gone and my father was standing there with a young nurse.

'My mother asked for the old nurse, only to be told the hospital did not employ older women. My mother became indignant and eventually the matron was called, who insisted the person my mother described did not work at the nursing home. The glass of water remained by my mother's bed and everyone denied bringing it.

'Within a very short time, my mother became pregnant with me. After my grandmother died, I went to my grandfather's house. My grandfather was rooting through their old possessions, looking for photographs of my grandmother. My mother came to collect me and suddenly started screaming, which was entirely out of character for her. She kept pointing at one of the old photographs and saying, "That's the old nurse, the old nurse I saw."

'My grandfather told her the picture was of his mother, who came from Barcelona.

'Although my parents were business people, my mother was still the wandering gypsy and she would take me on amazing adventures abroad. We once ended up in the hold of a ship with a man who was chained up because he had murdered his wife and children.

'Even now I get very restless if I live in the same place for long. My grandfather, too, hated being in houses for long and would go on long walks. When I was ten and he was 80, he took me on a walk from Wigan to St. Helen's, 17 miles or more, and carried me home on his back because I was tired.

'My first conscious psychic recollection is of travelling on a train from the French border to Barcelona with my mother, when I was about five years old. The Australian couple in the carriage with us became increasingly disturbed as I described in minute detail what was around every bend on every mile of the journey. How could I know as it was my first trip to

Spain? Barcelona was where my grandfather had been born and I was following the path home.

'When I about 13, my mother and I were staying in Palma, Majorca, and had made friends with a very charming French couple and their two children. We were booked on a flight home via Paris the next day. My mother had a feeling that the plane would crash and cancelled our tickets. To her horror, she discovered the French family were travelling on the same plane and begged them to change their tickets too. They disbelieved her, thinking she was being hysterical. The plane crashed and the whole family was killed.

'Not all my mother's premonitions were so doom-laden. In the summer of 1960, I had appeared in the BBC Sunday night drama in a play by Bill Norton. Then I flew to join my parents in Majorca for the holidays. We went to a cocktail party and my mother announced to the people to whom she was talking, "Of course, Jennifer won't be here next summer. Next year she will be famous and have a starring role in a television series that will run for a long time and be successful beyond anyone's wildest dreams.

'Of course, we thought she was away with the fairies. But I did only spend a short holiday with the family in Majorca the following year. Six months after my mother's prediction, I was offered the part of Lucille Hewitt in *Coronation Street*. The series is still running over 30 years later and is shown around the world.

'I knew the moment my own father died. He had been ill for some time with arterio-sclerosis. The illness went on and on and showed no signs of an end. One morning the telephone rang about 9.45-10 o'clock. I said to the woman who helped me with the children, "It's OK Mandy, I'll answer the phone. It's a call to tell me Daddy has just died."

'It was my mother's cleaner with that news. There was nothing unusual about receiving a call at that time of the morning. I just knew my father was gone. We had always been incredibly close.

'I have strong intuitive links with my grown-up daughter. We were estranged for a long time during her teenage years and at one point did not speak for three years. In 1989, my present husband Steve and I were due to go abroad. I needed a next-of-kin to put on my passport. I rang Naomi for the first time since the estrangement to ask what name she was using so I could put it on my passport. Then I said, "When's the baby due?"

' "How do you know I'm pregnant?" she asked indignantly and put the phone down on me.

'Seconds later the phone rang.

"You can't get rid of blood can you, Mum?" she said, and I think from that moment she realised we were still linked and that it is never too late to put things right. We are very happy now. I adore my grandchildren and Naomi gets on very well with Steve.

'To me my psychic roots are very important and show that families are linked in very deep ways whatever happens in life. It makes sense that those we love we can reach in times of need.'

Most premonitions and telepathic experiences involve family members and family crises, rather than strangers or global disasters. Yet because premonitions of earthquakes or plane crashes hit the headlines and tend to interest many researchers, the remarkable power of family love can be overlooked. As a result the prime movers of much psychic experience, family bonds, can be obscured. This book is an attempt to redress the balance.

Maternal intuition spans the spectrum of regularly waking in the night just before a baby stirs, to saving a child from a disaster there was no logical way of anticipating. The power of mother love is a remarkable example of paranormal ability in the everyday sphere. Even people who can't recall their psychic links with their own mother, may have a strong psychic bond with their own children. However, when a woman becomes a mother and starts to experience these things, her own mother may well recall, "Oh yes, I did that when you were small."

Often mothers take these abilities for granted, and it's not until the experiences are recounted to an outsider that the remarkable nature of the psychic link is realised. The bond seems to occur especially with mothers and a particular child who, whether three or 23, perhaps needs extra protection.

Dolores' psyche certainly had to work overtime with her

accident-prone teenager, although it was very disconcerting for Greg to discover that Mum 'knew' psychically when he was up to no good.

Dolores lives in California and works for a police department. All her psychic experiences have been centred around her immediate family – her late husband and son. The family now accepts and abides by Dolores' psychic guidance. Dolores listens to her sixth-sense and uses it, not to control the family, but in a positive way: 'When my son Greg was 16 and a half he begged his Dad and me for a moped. I did not want to buy him one, but his Dad gave in. One morning I warned Greg that I had had a very vivid dream. I had seen him riding double with a male friend I did not know, and he had had a fall. He laughed and said, "Not one of your dreams, Mom", though many had come true.

'Two weeks later I was at work interviewing a woman on the phone when I had a feeling of dread. It was almost as if a movie screen had come down in front of my face. I saw the accident I had seen previously in my dream. Greg fell off his moped and his head hit the cement. I could not see any blood and so I thought he was OK, although unconscious. Then I saw cars running over him.

'I did not know what to do but then I reasoned that if I could change the dream, it would be all right, if I could do anything, whistle, clap, sing, anything different from the dream ending. I put down the phone and got up and, strange though it sounds, started clapping to alter the tragic ending of the dream.

'Suddenly all the phones started ringing. There had been an accident in my home area. A young man was involved and I just knew it was Greg. The sergeant told me to relax as there were countless youths on mopeds. But I saw the vision again. This time I saw a van blocking the traffic, keeping the vehicles from trampling over Greg.

'The news came through that it was Greg involved in the accident. Greg was unconscious for 25 minutes. He had on heavy clothing which was ripped to shreds. He had a few scratches, but the main trauma was to his head. A van had stopped inches from his head and shielded him from the traffic. The nurses at the hospital could not believe how lucky he was to escape alive.'

But Greg did not learn to trust his mother's intuitions, or perhaps he hoped Dolores would continue to put things right psychically:

'On another occasion a boy across the street invited Greg to go jet ski-ing. Two weeks previously I had had another vivid dream about Greg drowning. I told Greg about it now and said he could go another time. But Greg waited until I had gone to work and went anyway. While I was at work, I got that dreadful feeling again and saw Greg go under the water as I had done in my dream. I could see his terrified eyes. His legs were cramped and he could not swim. I felt now as if I couldn't breathe. Then I saw something bite him on the shoulder – and blood.

'He was in the ocean and so my first fear was sharks. Then I realised it was a hand reaching for his tank top strap. When the hand pulled him above the surface, I took a deep breath as he did. I telephoned my home and my daughter answered. I asked where Greg was. She lied and told me he was down the street at his friend Geoff's house. I told her about my vision, which scared her. When her father came home she told him.

'My husband did not know exactly where Greg was so he waited till he came home and confronted him. Greg admitted he had gone jet ski-ing but would not say any more. My husband told Greg about my dream and vision. My son called me at work and admitted he had been in danger of drowning. I asked him if he had scratch marks on his shoulder where he had been rescued. He did, and said, "Mom, please don't do this to me," as the accident had happened exactly as I had seen.

'Greg's last psychic adventure concerned my classic 1964 Mustang convertible, which my son loved driving. I woke up one Tuesday morning, sweating and yelling. My husband was next to me and asked what was wrong. I told him that in my dream Greg had been in an accident in my car. On Saturday Greg asked to borrow my car. I warned him he would have an accident if he did. I told him that the accident would happen at the East/South Street corner where the moped accident had occurred. Greg was very upset but this time listened to me and agreed to get a lift with a friend instead. I took my car and drove to work. When I was almost at the corner of East/

South Street, I was thinking how I had changed the dream by not letting Greg take the car.

'Suddenly I had a very frightening feeling and felt intense cold. I looked up in time to see a car speeding into the road towards me. It was raining and I tried to turn left out of its way. However, it still hit me on the side and pushed my car on to the curb against a concrete post. It would have been even worse if I had not diverted, as the car would have hit me head on. I was squashed inside my car like a taco. I was able to open the convertible's top and get out. Had I borrowed my husband's car according to plan, I would not have been able to escape. I had minor cuts on my legs. The seat had pinned my shoulder and dislocated it. The car was ruined but I was spared. I believe that the crash was meant for Greg, but I altered the dream and took it on myself.'

Dolores had her first paranormal experience before her birth: "When my Mom was eight months pregnant with me she was sitting in the old women's sewing circle. Suddenly she and everyone there heard me cry inside her. I was not told this until I was 18.

'I have had dreams all my life. My husband died in May 1990. I went on vacation to Mexico in 1989. While I was in Mexico staying at my aunt's house, my sister, who was sleeping in a separate bed, was awakened by a sudden coldness in the room. She saw a misty figure going towards my bed. She screamed and the figure turned and smiled at her. It stroked my hair, and her second scream woke me. I was aware of an intense cold. The presence smiled, waved and disappeared. My aunt came in, but by that time all that she could see was the mist left by the figure on the floor.

'When I returned home, my husband told me he felt very ill and that he had dreamed he had died. This dream had occurred on the same day the figure appeared to my sister and myself. A week later my husband was diagnosed as having cancer. He died five months later. During his illness, he became very thin. His eyes became large and protruding. When my sister saw him she realised it was the person she had seen at my bedside.'

How can this psychic link work, whether it is a premonition or telepathy, not just with the mother and child but the whole family? It may be because the channels involved in paranormal events are those which are the strongest and most persistent in the family – love, and occasionally hatred. These emotions, like the gentle acceptance that seems to underlie everyday family telepathy, are rooted in years of sharing a home and lifestyle. The family psychic link is, as experiences demonstrate time and again, primarily one of love.

Ghosts, too, are more frequently loved family members than headless horsemen or Elizabethan ladies in white. A grandma may come back to see a new arrival; such manifestations are reassuring rather than spooky. A well-loved mother's perfume may be smelled at a time of crisis or loneliness. Above all, where a family member has died with guilt or unresolved anger, family ghosts can be immensely healing and suggest that the family link can be strengthened by death and that, as Jennifer Moss said, it is never too late to put things right.

Jane is a television producer. When she was 21 her father, with whom she had never got on, committed suicide. Suicide, above all manner of deaths, leaves those left behind with such a sense of guilt and anger that even grief becomes impossible. Jane was staying at a health farm some time after her father's death when she met a medium who told her that her father was still with her and wanted her to know he had not meant to do it. Jane refused to believe the woman, and said if her father had come back, he must give proof. The medium said, "Tell your mother she has lost something precious and that she will find it in the back pocket of the old brown suitcase in her bedroom."

Jane still doubted the validity of the experience, as her mother had not mentioned losing anything. However, next time Jane saw her mother she did ask if there was an old brown suitcase in her bedroom. There was, not in itself surprising since such cases were very common 30 years ago. Jane told her mother to look in the back pocket but did not say why.

Jane's mother did so, and to her intense joy found the engagement ring she had lost. Jane's mother explained that she had mislaid the ring and searched everywhere for it as it was a memento of happier times. Jane's father had appeared

to her several times asking why she had lost their engagement ring. However, he refused to say where it was, only that
he would tell someone else where it could be found.

Jane has only seen her father once, though she has known
he is around on many occasions. She and her husband Nick
went on holiday to Northumberland with a couple of friends.
One day they went for a walk. It was the anniversary of Jane's
father's death. Jane explained: 'I was sitting on a bank when
suddenly I saw my father – it is the only time I have ever
actually seen him. He took my hand, "Come on, we have to
talk," he said, and with a whoosh I found myself flying
through the air, holding his hand until we landed on a high
hill a long way away. I can remember the two of us talking,
and though I don't recall on a conscious level what he said, on
a deeper level I understood, and for the first time I was at
peace and knew my father loved me.

'I found myself walking back along a path – it must have
been two and a half hours later – to find my husband and my
friends who had been frantically looking for me. I had just
disappeared and they had been walking round calling my
name. The next day we were amazed to see how far I had
travelled. It was not the kind of weather to go off alone, and
when I saw the path I realised I might have fallen over a
cliff.'

Jane moved to a rented house in Gloucestershire when she
had her child Georgia. At about nine months old, Georgia
would wake screaming and point to the end of the bed,
screaming, 'Mummy!' There was a strange atmosphere in the
house. Drawers would tip and things break. Jane explained
this away as a result of the uneven floors.

One night when Jane tried to go upstairs she found she
could not open the door to the upper floor. Suddenly the
door blew open and there was a cold, rushing wind and a
voice saying, 'You cannot come up here.'

Since Jane's husband was away, Jane slept downstairs with
Georgia, and unusually her daughter slept right through the
night. All night there was bumping and banging, objects
being thrown, and cries. Jane lay awake all night. In the morning the door opened easily and the atmosphere was completely different. Jane could smell her father's distinctive

smell – tobacco and wood-smoke. What is more the house felt totally peaceful. The poltergeist had gone and Georgia slept undisturbed thereafter. It was as if Jane's father had protected her as he had never done in life, and sent whatever was menacing the family away. A few weeks later Jane discovered that a young woman who had lived in the house many years before had hanged herself in the room Georgia slept in.

'We have sensed my father in all our subsequent homes for a while, as if he is making sure we are safe. I was in a very bad car crash a few years ago. The car turned over and I found myself in my seat belt, upside down, I heard my father's voice persistently, "Undo your seat belt and get out of the car", on and on until I responded. He saved my life.

'When Georgia was born she was big and apparently healthy but my father's voice went on and on, "Call the doctor" in my head, until we did. Georgia had a collapsed lung.

'The most recent time I knew my father was there was a recent Christmas Eve in church. I got a fit of the giggles and Nick asked me why I was laughing. My father was standing next to me, singing out of tune. I now see him in my mind's eye rather than with my physical senses. It is hard to explain, but the relationship is right at last.

Out-of-body experiences, too, are often prompted by family concerns. Usually people leave their bodies, not just to go walkabout but to visit family members far away, who may be in distress. Sometimes, however, they want to check nothing untoward is happening in their absence. The people they visit may be aware of the living ghost.

Love, perhaps tinged with the green-eyed monster, prompted Doris's astral trip from Australia to Bromley in Kent to check that her little house was being cared by her sister-in-law Madge and that Ron, the widower next door, whom Doris hoped to marry, wasn't also being too well tended by the widowed Madge:

'I'd gone to Australia to visit relations. I woke about eight in the morning as usual and suddenly there was a rushing noise and I found myself in the sky going a long way, and I passed from light to darkness. Suddenly, to my amazement, I was back in my very own front hall in Bromley – Madge my sister-in-law, was staying there while I was away. Ron, my next-door neighbour and very dear friend, was standing there and the sitting room door was half open. I didn't want to push open the sitting room door because I thought it might scare them.

'I wonder if I could walk through the wall?' I said to myself, and I found I could. I was standing in a corner of the room. Ron was in front of the fireplace looking at the *Radio Times*. He said to Madge, "It's nearly ten o' clock. I don't want to miss the news."

"I'm feeling pretty tired," Madge replied. "Besides, it's always so depressing to watch, never any good news."

"I'll go next door now. Why don't you have an early night?"

"I'm sure Doris is here," my sister-in-law said suddenly.

"Yes, she is," Ron said. "I can feel her. Maybe she's thinking of us."

'I hugged them both. It was dark outside and I went back through the darkness into the light – after making sure they went their separate ways. I'd hardly touched the pillow when my nephew was there telling me it was time to get up as we were going on an outing.

'Later I phoned my sister-in-law and found out it wasn't a dream, but had all happened as I saw. And not long after my return I married Ron before somebody else snapped him up.'

As I mentioned in the Introduction, it has been argued by some psychologists with whom I talked that a psychic family, i.e. one where psychic experience is accepted and even encouraged, is an unhealthy one because it excludes the outside world and can be a power ploy by one parent, usually the mother, to keep her children close and shut out her husband and the outside world. Psychic links, like more earthly bonds, can be used to keep family members unduly dependent. When this happens the effect can be devastating. The following story shows how a dead matriarch reasserted her control over her son. Yet had she not lived on in his mind and exerted an unconscious control, the incident would not have had such potency. Often bad psychic experiences are rooted in unresolved past conflicts in close relationships.

Thelma, a widow in her seventies who lives on a neat estate of retirement bungalows on the Isle of Wight, told me how in

1917 her own father was persuaded to attend a large spiritualist meeting in Detroit. He was very reluctant to go and only went so he would not offend his hostess. His worst suspicions were confirmed as he gazed at the rapt audience, and he stood up to leave. At that moment the medium came on to the platform and said, 'I have a message for the gentleman by the door.

"Oh, Willy, I did miss you."'

Thelma's father was devastated. She explained: 'My father burst into tears because that was what his deceased mother used to say to him when he came home late as a little boy. She never scolded him but by telling him she had missed him she made him feel guilty and kept him under her thumb.'

Thelma told me that her father was so eager to hear his mother's voice again – for he was convinced it was her voice which had come through the medium – that he went out and bought all the paraphernalia. He desperately tried to persuade friends to hold seances with him. But he never heard his mother's voice again, and his obsession caused difficulties with his wife.

Living or dead, one family member should not control the lives of others. Usually, however, possessiveness tends to kill off intuition and discourages family psychic links.

The link of love is perhaps the best explanation for most telepathic experiences, and so I start with the maternal bond – the most common, exciting and least researched area of psychic experience.

# 2

---

# THE MATERNAL LINK OF LOVE

The power of maternal love is legendary. A widowed squaw and her young son lived by the sea in eastern Canada. One day the boy went to hunt beavers, but was seized by the great eagle which carried him off to its nest on a high cliff overlooking the sea, to feed its young. First the eagles ate the beaver the boy had killed, while he lay in terror in the nest waiting his turn to be devoured.

At home his mother wept for him, but an old woman who had learned the secrets of the fairies said to her: 'Little good the men of your tribe can do you. You must aid him with your thoughts, for material things are in vain.'

That night, when the boy slept, his mother came to him in his dreams and said: 'Tomorrow when the great eagle swoops down to kill you, brace your knife, point upwards against the rock and he will be pierced to death. You are not strong enough to cut through his feathers, but he is powerful enough to destroy himself.' The boy did as he was told and the eagle was impaled. Then he killed the young eagles, but could see no way to escape from the nest.

That night his mother again came to him in a dream and said: 'Foolish boy, why do you not use the thoughts I send you? Skin the eagle, then crawl inside his skin. If the wide wings can hold him in the air they can likewise hold you. Drop from the cliff and you will land safely on the beach.'

Thus the boy escaped, and back at his village boasted of his strength and cunning. But the wise old woman said: 'O vain boy, do not think so highly of yourself. Your strength is nothing, your shrewdness is nothing. It was not these that saved you but the strength of your mother's thoughts.'

In real life, too, the maternal link can be a lifesaver and is the most central of family psychic bonds. It seems that even if a mother is far from her child she can send her love to protect him or her. That sounds fanciful, but according to many women I have spoken to, has worked in real-life crises. It is far more common than I had believed and though this power does exist between husband and wife, seems most prevalent in the mother/child situation.

I met Judi in Los Angeles and heard how her prayers had, she believed, saved her son Corey as his life was threatened in a potentially fatal motorbike accident. Her experience is the more remarkable since Judi thought Corey was safely in school as usual. What is more Corey did not even possess a motorbike:

'It was in May 1989, about two weeks before the dismissal of school for the summer. The seniors were going to celebrate Senior Skip Day, which I knew nothing about. Corey, along with many of his classmates, had planned to skip school that day to have a party at the country home of a friend who had graduated the previous year. Corey had borrowed a motorbike from his older brother, Cris, which I also did not know.

'Around noon, as I was standing in my kitchen looking out of the window, I was suddenly filled with intense fear and immediately thought of Corey. I told myself this was ridiculous because I knew Corey was in school and was just fine. But the feeling grew stronger and I began shaking and crying uncontrollably. Then my mind was filled with the words: "Pray for Corey." I did not hear the words with my physical ear, but the feelings were so intense I could not ignore them and I stood there shaking and praying to God that He would surround Corey with his love and protection. When I was able to calm myself I went into the living room and sat on the sofa, still shaking, trying to understand what had happened to me.

'Ten minutes later the telephone rang. It was Corey's best friend telling me Corey had just been involved in a motor-cycle accident. The emergency services had been called to transport him to hospital although he had not been badly hurt. I ran next door and got my father to come to the hospital with me because I was so afraid of what I would find when I got there.

'While Corey was in X-ray, the deputy sheriff, who had investigated the accident, arrived in the emergency room and talked with me. He said Corey definitely had his guardian angel with him in the crash. As Corey rounded a curve in the highway, the back tyre of his motorcycle hit loose gravel which caused him to lose control of the vehicle, throwing the motorcycle across the highway and Corey into a small ditch running along the side of the road. Corey travelled along the ditch on his stomach, passing directly between a cement culvert and a pile of rocks. If Corey had veered even a couple of inches in either direction he surely would have been killed. After passing between the culvert and the rocks, Corey then rolled on to the highway into the path of an oncoming truck. Because the truck driver was alert and had seen what was happening he had slowed the truck or he would have hit Corey.

'There was nothing left of the motorcycle but the gas tank. Corey sustained minor injuries for what he had just gone through – a cracked clavicle and abrasions to his hands and his face from which he has no scars. As near as I can figure I was having my experience just as Corey was involved in the accident.

'Only one other time did I have a telepathic experience with Corey. After graduation from high school, Corey went into the US Army and was stationed in Germany for his first Christmas away from home. During that Christmas, for three days, I had a terrible sore throat. This was unusual because I never get sore throats, having had my tonsils removed as a young girl. I could not understand why I was having so much trouble. I could barely swallow. A couple of days after Christmas, Corey telephoned home to say he had just been dismissed from hospital. He had been hospitalised because he had suffered a "strep" throat and couldn't swallow for three days.

'I knew then why my throat had been bothering me so much.'

How can this link work? Is it because the child was part of the mother for nine months, or that a mother can somehow galvanise a child's own survival mechanism into overdrive? Or does she send actual strength whether though her prayers or through love?

Answers are few, for the situation cannot be recreated to the satisfaction of scientists. Nor do mothers write down or tell outsiders of their experience as it is occurring. When a child's life is at stake, being of benefit to the learned community is low on a list of priorities. Yet to dismiss such experiences as coincidence does sell short the value of human experience. Jude said it was the only time she had such a feeling, and many mothers who experience crisis telepathy, whether they are able to go to a child or simply send love, do speak of this unique, urgent, over-riding sensation.

I met Susan in less exotic surroundings, at a talk I was giving in Bournemouth on the south coast of England, and she told me the following story from her family history:

'My uncle was serving on HMS *Hood* during the war. One night my gran woke and heard my uncle calling for help. She prayed for him. The next day she heard the ship had gone down and my uncle was one of the few survivors.'

Where does this maternal link begin? The crucial stage for the mother-bond seems to be that time before the child can speak for itself and sometimes cannot even cry out to show its distress. Anne from Leicestershire, a La Lèche leader and mother of five children, wrote to me:

'My fifth daughter was just nine days old. I had put her down peacefully asleep in her Moses basket on the dining room table and went to do something else in another part of the house. A very short time later I was walking through the room and had no reason to check her as she was obviously sleeping peacefully.

'But for some reason I was compelled to go over to the

basket, and saw her silently choking. I can't say that it was anything more than "mother's instinct". I know my mother was at the house with me and all afternoon we were commenting on fate and that if I hadn't checked her at that moment she may well have choked to death. It certainly struck us strongly that it was amazing that I had felt drawn to look at her at that moment when there was no apparent reason to do so.

'I'd had the same experience several times with my third child who was born prematurely and who, on a number of occasions, appeared to stop breathing. This instinct for going to him at these times carried on for quite a while. I remember when he was just about three months and had not long been sleeping in his own room when suddenly I felt I had to go to his room and check him. As I looked I realised he was not breathing. I quickly shook his arm and he started and took a breath. If I had not gone in I don't know what may have happened.'

Sceptics argue that a mother unconsciously hears the absence of breathing – in itself pretty remarkable. But the fact is that most mothers are not leaping up every five seconds checking. In Anne's case she was not even a first-time mother, when anxiety is at its greatest. The key factor is that the mother does not wonder if the baby is OK. If she has time to reflect then probably there is not an emergency. This psychic call is urgent and the mother responds automatically. What is more, it occurs even when the baby is in a different room. According to Sandra, this maternal link averted what would otherwise have been a cot death:

'When Katie was six and a half weeks old, she was quite dozy one day where normally she was demanding. The health visitor had been in for a minor problem and declared everything was fine. But all day I felt something was going to happen and I had the irrational thought, "If something's going to happen with the baby, I'd rather it happened now than later." My husband Geoff put her to bed and she settled straight down.

'But I still felt uneasy. I went into her room, switched on the light and she blinked. I nearly went out but I went back again to her. Thirty seconds later she had stopped breathing. The doctor said she had been a near cot death and we were in hospital for eight days while she was checked over. I have never felt like that before or since. The hospital could find no reason why it had happened. I am very close to Katie, maybe because I breastfed her.'

Joanne also believes her nine-week-old son James was saved by the psychic link between them: 'I took James to a friend's house. She had two toddlers so we put James upstairs for his sleep. My friend checked him and came down. But I felt I had to check him again almost straight away. When I went in, he was turning navy blue. I only just saved him. He has been given an experimental alarm that detects the blood oxygen level, an earlier stage of detection than breathing, which is the last thing to go.'

On several occasions, Joanne says she has been impelled to check him and has gone in his room just before the alarm went off.

Often a mother will go to a child at a time when logically there is no need, and yet this may be the very time he or she needs help. I have met mothers who have felt they must go to a baby when they are having a bath and the taps would drown out all sound and, perhaps most remarkable, a case where the baby was apparently safe with her father.

Carolyn from Salt Lake City was in the kitchen when she had the blinding flash that eight-month-old Sarah was choking. She rushed to the living room where her husband was reading and her older daughter was playing. The baby was lying in the corner apparently quite happy. But when Carolyn flipped her over, Sarah was silently choking on a balloon. I wrote about Carolyn's experience in my book, *A Mother's Instincts*, but still cannot explain it away logically.

Even with an older child, the maternal instinct may be more efficient than the latest technology. Rebecca wrote to me last year from Hampshire:

'I first heard your name years ago, when the sister of the ward where my daughter Leonie was staying mentioned your research. The staff were fascinated by the entirely natural phenomenon of a mother's telepathy with her child.

'My child would stop breathing unexpectedly, and I always

woke or knew it was happening even if I was not by her. It always seemed surprising to me that everyone found it remarkable – as if I would not know when my daughter was suffocating. The staff found I was more reliable as a warning than their machines, and so we managed without. At Leonie's death, two years ago at the age of eight, I sat with her, willing her to go, telling her it was all right to be whole and well again, and all the time feeling as if my heart would stop when hers did.'

Some health professionals do find it hard to accept maternal instinct. One eminent obstetrician described maternal instinct as a primitive mechanism that could encourage mothers to have delusions of expertise. However, Jane, a health professional who works extensively with mothers and babies in the home counties, says that because maternal experiences are not well documented or researched, and worse still not acknowledged, a valuable warning system for babies' health could be lost:

'Mothers may suddenly feel that they must go to their baby, even though they may have left the child with their partner or a perfectly reliable babysitter and gone off for just a short time, glad of the break'.

Helena, a breastfeeding counsellor with the La Lèche League, who lives in Berkshire, had such an experience. She told me how when her second child Amy was a few months old, her husband Chris persuaded her to go out for a couple of hours to see some friends for dinner. The babysitter was left with the number to call in case of any emergency and the couple could be back home within a few minutes:

'When it got to about 10, we were sitting around talking and my attention started to wander. I started to get agitated. I really think we ought to be going,' I insisted.

Chris said, 'Well, the babysitter's got our number here if there's any problem.'

But Helena had to get back as quickly as possible. She cannot remember how they got out. She felt cut off from the outside world, thinking only, 'I want to get back to my baby.'

They reached home to find baby crying and the babysitter trying frantically to phone them – Chris had accidentally written two of the numbers in the wrong order.

Though many mothers do not have life and death experiences with their babies – though quite a number do – most women recall how they would wake in the night before the baby, even if he or she was in another room and had no regular waking pattern. This phenomenon is so common as to be disregarded, and yet it is perhaps the most exciting example of mother/child bonding and one we should rejoice in.

It can be distressing for a mother to link in with her child when she cannot comfort him, but some doctors do not recognise that excluding a mother from surgical or medical procedures may upset both the child and absent mother, rather than saving her pain. Caroline from Ontario recalled:

'After the Caesarean birth of my first born, the doctor told me that he would circumcise my son on a particular day. That morning I decided to shower. When I was in the shower I heard my baby cry. This was physically impossible, since the water was running and I was at the opposite end of the hospital to the nursery. I hurried up and as I walked out of the shower a nurse walked up and asked if I had spoken to the doctor who was looking for me. I said I had not, and she proceeded to tell me that my son had been circumcised while I was in the shower. I know that I did hear him, but not with my ears. I think that motherhood has increased my psychic vibes.'

Breastfeeding is often a factor because obviously if it is right for the mother and baby then it is a very natural form of feeding. But bottle-feeding mothers experience the same links. The mother link is one of love, not hormones or genes alone. In Chapter 9 adoptive mothers speak of the psychic link with children who did not spring from their bodies.

The maternal link remains throughout the child's life, though it lessens as a child can operate his or her own awareness of danger. At the beginning of this chapter Jude explained how she linked into her teenage son's distress, and at times of danger to their child mothers of teenagers do regain that early radar system. Throughout the other chapters in the book are many examples of this maternal link, even into adulthood.

On an everyday level, many people recall that they go to

telephone mum at the exact moment she is dialling their number, again when there is no regular pattern of contact. Or Mum may phone from hundreds or even thousands of miles away to ask what's wrong, whether it's a bad cold or a broken heart. Again we tend to feel "Oh, everyone does that." They do, and this is an exciting demonstration that the psychic bond is not just for a privileged few but exists in all our lives in connection with those we care for.

Indeed, Thelma explained how one day she rang her daughter Sylvia, who was living on the Isle of Wight, from Hong Kong, where Thelma had her home:

'I dialled the code for England and began to dial the Isle of Wight code. But before I could do so I heard Sylvia's voice. "Mum, is that you?" She had started to dial my number and we connected. We didn't have a regular day or time to phone, but we'd been thinking about each other quite strongly prior to the call.'

As the child becomes older the communication becomes two-way, and a mother can pick up on her mother's distress from far away.

Julia lives in Weymouth. She told me how she linked into her mother's distress hundreds of miles away. As in so many cases her mother had not wanted to worry her, not realising that the psychic link of love would alert Julia anyway:

'When I was 17 I moved with my family to Holland. When I was 19 I decided to return to England and moved in with my gran in Bolton. My mum always phoned either on Monday or Tuesday night between 5 and 6 o'clock. One Monday I said to my nan, "Mum won't phone. There's something wrong." My gran tried to reassure me by saying it was early and she would probably phone the next day.

'I told my gran that my dad, not my mum, would phone tomorrow, though he was never the one to call, because there was something wrong with my mum and she could not manage it.

'The following day it was my father who phoned. He told me my mother was in hospital recovering from a mastectomy due to cancer. She had had the operation on Monday. Unfortunately she died less than two years later. That was 10 years ago.'

Jacqui from Shepperton explained how she has on several occasions picked up her mother's distress though she, too, is far away:

'I am very close to my mother, although I don't see a lot of her these days. There have been numerous occasions when we have both picked up the telephone at the same time. But more remarkable is the number of times I have known when something has been wrong. For example, she went to wake my 16-year-old brother one morning to find him dead in bed. Shortly afterwards I had this overwhelming compulsion to telephone her, as I just knew there was something dreadfully wrong.

'On another occasion she went into hospital, but told me she was going away for a few days so as not to worry me. However, again I felt instinctively this wasn't the case and forced her to confess.

'My grandmother, to whom I was also very close, was seriously ill in hospital. My mother did not leave her side for several days. I went in and out of the hospital during that period, and one time went home to make sandwiches to take back to my mother. While I was making them I suddenly heard my grandmother's voice saying, "It's all right, Jacqui."

'When I returned to the hospital I discovered my grandmother had died'.

Of course, if mum is kicking over the traces, a daughter's psychic intervention can prove embarrassing. Theresa, who lives in Londonderry, told me of a dream that linked her with her mother:

'In my dream my mother was sitting on the side of my bed telling me that she needed a man in her life. The reason I found this dream so strange was that in the nine years my mother has been divorced she has not even considered going out with anyone. She is a devout Christian and believes that marriage is for life.

'The next day I was at my mother's for lunch and in passing asked her if she had been out anywhere interesting the night before. To my astonishment she said, "Yes, I was out with a man called David, and I had a lovely time." I nearly choked on my tea.'

I have come across men who have the same kind of links

with their mother, but when I get down to questioning they tend to shuffle, look at their feet and claim not to remember any specific details. If any male reader would send me their experiences I will print them in my next book and take back this statement.

Perhaps the most fascinating aspect of the mother/child bond is the ability of a small child to read a mother's mind. Jo, from Nottingham, also regularly experiences her daughter Hannah's mind-hopping:

'My daughter Hannah seems to read my thoughts, but it is always at a time of complete subconsciousness, i.e. we can't make it happen. One instance was when my husband was fixing the car. I was sitting on the bonnet of the car and Hannah was inside the car. I was thinking about age and about my parents getting older. Hannah wound the window down and said, "Grandad's not old."

'I asked her why she said that and she told me she just saw it. Hannah was about three years old at the time.

'There have been lots of times when I have been in one room wondering to myself whether Hannah would like something to eat and she shouts "Yes please," or "No thank you, mummy."

'One morning I was lying in bed. Hannah had got into bed next to me and Andrew my husband was getting dressed. Andrew made us laugh and I thought, "Silly twit."

'Hannah said, "Don't be rude, mummy."

"What do you mean?", I asked.

"Andrew's not silly."'

Fathers, especially those who spend a lot of time just being with a child and caring for him or her on a routine level, also have this everyday link. I describe this in the next chapter. Again, however, fathers are under-represented in my research, although men do listen to the radio programmes on which I appear. It may simply be reticence in coming forward, or perhaps many men still don't get a chance to spend time with small children doing the mundane tasks. I would love to know the answer.

I don't have a label for the phenomenon of a small child knowing his or her mother is pregnant before she does. It is not a premonition, but it certainly beats even the most expensive pregnancy test.

Lin, who lives in Essex, described how her son Steven knew she was pregnant before she did:

'When Steven was four years old, he and his big sister Lucy were having a rough and tumble with me on the bed. Lucy was jumping all over me and it was getting quite boisterous, when Steven said to her, quite out of the blue, "Be careful, mummy's got a baby in her tummy."

'His words shook me, as my husband and I had been trying for a baby for only two weeks and it had been a complete and utter secret. I told my husband and mum and dad and we laughed at what he had said. Two weeks later I discovered Steven's uncanny prediction had come true – another beautiful daughter. I'm a little uncertain of his uncanny foresight these days as my husband has since had a vasectomy!'

The saddest telepathic experiences occur when a mother loses a child and links in with his or her death. Yet perhaps it is a sign of the deep, abiding love that exists. I am very grateful that in spite of some very close shaves, I have my children alive, well and thoroughly annoying. Jennice, from Accrington, explained her psychic link with her baby daughter that began from early on and was a comfort when she did eventually lose her child, as the bond seemed to carry on:

'When my daughter Dee was about seven months old I was working in the evening and my husband was bathing Dee when there was an accident. Dee poured hot water on her foot.

'Meanwhile I was working making wire harnesses, and suddenly the board I was working on seemed to come towards me. After that I had an overwhelming compulsion to go home. My friend kept asking if I was OK as apparently I went white. But I felt fine in myself. I just felt I was needed at home for Dee.

'Then suddenly my husband was there telling me to get a pass out and come home quickly. He was waiting outside in the car with Dee with a bandaged foot. It was at the exact time that the board appeared to move that Dee had scalded her foot'.

'Dee and I had a very close relationship. When Dee was small and learning to talk, which took longer than usual because she had Down's Syndrome, I could hold a very involved conversation because I knew instinctively what she was trying to say to me. My husband just did not have a clue what she wanted and sometimes they would both get very frustrated. As the years went on we became very close and I could tell what mood she was in, sometimes even before I woke her up in the morning.

'When Dee was 12 years old leukaemia was diagnosed. She battled for nearly two years, but she died on Christmas Day 1990. But she is still here with us. She used to play with and lose my husband's keys. Since Dee died, he still loses them and asks her to find them. They usually turn up somewhere we have already looked.

'He once lost his wallet and shortly afterwards the keys went missing. He got rather annoyed, but nothing was found so he went out to clean the car. Next time he came into the lounge the wallet was on the chair arm. He then went to change out of his old trainers. He put his foot into his shoes and there were the keys inside one of them.

'When Dee went into hospital for the last time, it was the beginning of December and I thought I would put up the tree a bit early, thinking it would encourage her to want to get better and come home. When I told her she screamed, "Take it down," so I never mentioned it again, not to her or to anyone else.

'About three months after she died, my sister's friend went to see a medium who could see a child and also an initial 'D'. When my sister told me, I just didn't know what to think. Then, in about September 1994, my mother-in-law saw Dee at the bottom of her bed in the night. Dee was wondering where the tree was. So this Christmas, for the first time since Dee died, I put up that tree, and looking back over Christmas I felt more settled and Christmas seemed much easier. I wonder, does Dee feel more at peace?'

When an adult child dies, the pain is overwhelming and may even be experienced physically. Sandra woke in the middle of the night with the most terrible pain in her stomach. She staggered to the bathroom next to her bedroom, but by the time she got there the pain had vanished. A few hours later, her son, Gifford, just a few weeks short of his eighteenth birthday, was involved in an accident on his motorbike. He came off and was hit in the stomach by a road sign.

He was dead on arrival in hospital.

Sandra was devastated, but she took some comfort from the belief that if the terrible pain she had experienced a few hours earlier had only lasted a few seconds, her son had only suffered for a very short time.

Gifford's elder sister, who told me the story, said that often there is the very real worry that though doctors may say a person only suffered for a very short time, they may just be saying that for the benefit of the relatives.

Gifford had a twin sister, and throughout childhood whenever Gifford, who was just 10 minutes older, had an accident, one for Sharon would follow within a short time. Two weeks later, Sharon was a passenger in a car which was hit from behind at a roundabout. Fortunately, she was unhurt.

Did Sandra share her son's pain in advance? She had no premonition of disaster and no inkling of why she suffered a sudden and passing agony.

The maternal bond does, as I said earlier, become a two-way process as children grow older. But children, whether teenage or adult, can link into the death of their mother. In a later chapter I talk about these bonds with grandparents, but there is a special pain in losing one's mother, at whatever age. Twenty-five years on I still miss mine desperately.

Helen knew her mother had died even though her husband tried to wait for the right moment to break the news:

'One morning I had a dreadful feeling of foreboding, and I went to the corner shop to buy the first edition of the local paper. In the "Stop Press" were the words "Old lady killed in High Street at 10 a.m.", and I knew it was my mother.

'My husband came home early at lunchtime. He was a policeman at the local station and if he got time off always brought the local paper home to read with his dinner. I asked him if he had bought it as usual, because I knew he would have received the news of Mum. He told me he'd not had time to get a paper.

'I said, "Mum's been killed in the High Street, hasn't she? I read it in the paper".

'"How could you know it was your mother?" he asked. "No details have been released till all the relatives could be contacted. I was going to wait for the right moment to tell you."'

# 3

# FAMILY TELEPATHY

The psychic bonds of love are not purely those of blood. Next to the maternal/child link, the strongest bond is usually that between partners. If the couple is childless, the psychic connections can be very concentrated. Couples say that they finish each other's sentences and anticipate the other's needs, which may be rooted in familiarity and fondness. However, even deeper can be links that need explanation beyond logic. At its most dramatic, husband/wife or partner telepathy can be a lifesaver.

I found Adrian's story in an old pile of records. He recalled:

'In 1917 I was piloting an Avro aeroplane in the Royal Flying Corps at Dover, and I switched off the engine to glide down. The plane entered a strong wind from the sea and was blown into a flat spinning nose-dive, and this I knew to be fatal. I switched on the engine, and to my horror it failed to start up. I realised that in another moment the plane would crash and I would become pulp and ashes. I thought of my wife Rose and she loomed up before me and instantly the engine started up again.

'The very next morning I received a letter from my wife asking if something terrible had happened to me as she was suddenly moved to go down on her knees and pray for me. The time she mentioned coincided with the time she loomed up before me, when I believed I was about to be killed.'

Wartime is so fraught with peril that everyday concerns fade and we seem able more easily to tap our inner powers, or as believers interpret such intervention, external help from God. Such marital psychic experiences are frequent in peacetime too, when even those who don't go to church regularly may turn to prayer in crisis. Whether it is a deity or the power of goodness that responds, or our own inner magic, the results affirm that love can conquer danger, and partners pick up the other's distress.

Tricia, a Southampton businesswoman, has been married for 27 years and also works with her husband. She recounted how her intuition probably saved her husband's life:

'I know my husband Ken as well as I know myself. I had been ill at home with back trouble for five months. One lunchtime my husband came home. Ken was distracted and not at all himself, but he insisted on going back to work. Half an hour later he came home, saying he did not feel well, and he looked ill. I just knew Ken was having a heart attack, though he did not have any chest pain or what are considered any of the classic symptoms of heart trouble, only a very stiff neck. I rang my son as I could not drive. I did not want to frighten him by saying his father was having a heart attack, so I explained we needed to go to the doctor at once.

'The receptionist was very unhelpful and made us wait, even though I told her my husband was getting worse. At last we saw the doctor who examined Ken and diagnosed that he had indigestion and should take some brand tablets. I am not easily roused to anger, but I insisted that I knew my husband was having a heart attack and I was taking him to the hospital at once. At this point the doctor agreed to give me a note of referral to allay my fears.

'We drove straight to casualty and Ken was admitted at once suffering from a heart attack. He was put into intensive care and was in hospital for several weeks.

'A doctor later said that had I not taken my husband to hospital when I did he would probably have died on the way. This doctor told me that heart attack cases do not necessarily

display what are regarded as classic symptoms, but I no longer wished to trust my GP with our health.'

We may often say to a family member who is in pain, 'I wish
I could bear it for you'. The late C. S. Lewis, the Oxford
philosopher who was perhaps loved most for his *Narnia*
children's books, believed that he did bear part of the pain for
his wife Joy, who was suffering from secondary cancer of the
bone. They were married for only three years and four months, but for C. S. Lewis, in spite of her illness, it was the happiest time of his life. During the early weeks of 1957, when
Joy Lewis believed she was dying, her husband prayed to be
allowed to take on some of her suffering.

By the end of April, Joy, who had been immobile, found
herself able to move around the house and even go on
outings. Her husband, however, was diagnosed as suffering
from osteoporosis, thinning of the bones, because of a loss of
calcium. To the end of his days C. S. Lewis was convinced that
as he lost calcium Joy had been absorbing it, and that gave
them the brief time of happiness together.

Yet it is not the existence of legal ties that causes these links.
Some people do believe that marriage provides the stability
where such feelings can more easily grow. But there are close
links between lovers and former lovers that survive separation and even new partners. Elaine's experience is just one
example of an unbroken love link. Elaine, who lives in Utah,
told me:

'There was a fellow I had known since I was 14. We had
dated over 10 years but never married. John had finally
married a girl he had met in the Philippines and was travelling with her to various islands before they were to return to
live in Alaska, where he worked and lived. All during that
month I had very good feelings that he was finally happy
and settled.

'One night, however, I woke up and could hardly breathe.
My side hurt and I was panicking. After walking around the
house and catching my breath I lay back in bed to try to figure
out what was going on. I was sure something had happened
to John.

'At the same time John's mother (who lives in another
state) woke up with a pain in her side and knew that her son

was dead. She was notified that John, his wife and father, had
been shot by rebels. John had been killed by gunshot wounds
to his side.'

Not all links between couples are so dramatic. Much of the
telepathic communication between partners concerns everyday issues.

Jackie, from San Diego, USA, recalled the telepathic link
she had with her long-standing love:

'For many years, over and over again, Douglas, the man I
went out with for over 15 years, would be calling me at the
same time I was trying to locate him. He travelled constantly
for a telephone company and I would have to call the main
office to locate Douglas. This usually took some time, as they
were a day behind with their information.

When Douglas rang, at the same moment my line would be
busy as I was dialling him. Sometimes I had not heard from
him previously for five or six months. My own analysis is that
I did want him very much to be my own permanently, and
was therefore sensitive to him even when we were miles
apart'.

June, who lives in Birmingham, told me that she has had a
close man friend for 15 years, and that he always knows if she
is ill or unhappy. June is also linked to George:

'I once had a terribly strong urge to phone George. He
answered and I said, "You're being taken into hospital
aren't you?"

'He admitted that he had started spitting up blood and was
being admitted almost immediately. Although cancer was
diagnosed, I knew he would get better. I think it helped him
as he knew I was always right about such things. He does still
have problems and I will wake at 2 a.m and know if he is
struggling to get breath. I can feel if he can't sleep. Once he
had gone to sit in the churchyard in the middle of the night,
and I woke up and knew he was wandering around the
streets in the dark. It can be very bad for my beauty sleep, but
I suppose it is inevitable and it shows we are close, so I
am glad.'

In my own marriage, my husband John is not a great one
for flowers and phone calls, psychic or otherwise, to say 'I
love you'. Our psychic communication has reflected the more

downbeat nature of our relationship, and like our earthly contact has centred on blocked drains and missed buses. During the summer of 1989, while living in Reading, I dropped my husband at a bus stop near Maidenhead after the usual last-minute panic to catch an express coach into London. John's missing the coach and my hot pursuit were frequent impromptu family  outings. Any concern on my part was overcome by the children's demands to go home to finish their lunch or watch *Sesame Street*.

However, on this occasion, as soon as I walked through the front door I said to the children, "We'd better go back. Your father's having transport problems."

This didn't strike me as odd until we were driving along the A4 towards the bus stop, but I reasoned that maybe the bus hadn't turned up. The bus stop was deserted. I carried on up the A4 to find a turn-off, and not a mile up the road was the broken-down coach with my husband sitting gloomily on the top deck.

In practice I had not helped, but the fact is that I did not normally either wait to see that John was on the bus or feel impelled to go and check. This is perhaps the key factor in telepathic experiences, that a person does act either apparently against logic or normal routine, and go to a partner or link into him or her urgently.

On another occasion I was due to meet John after work in the car at the Albert Memorial in Kensington. As I pulled up he wasn't there – no surprise, since time-keeping isn't John's greatest strength. But I suddenly thought, 'I've got a long wait. All the lights have gone out.'

They hadn't, but I did have a long, tedious wait. When John eventually arrived he said, "You'll not believe this. The bus was going down Oxford Street when the lights on the top deck failed, and we had to wait while they were fixed."

That had been at the time of my apparently irrational thought about the lights. Maybe I picked up John's thoughts, or perhaps he picked up mine and so found an excuse I'd be sure to believe. Telepathy either way.

When a couple have been together more than half a lifetime, it is not surprising that they are joined on the deepest level. Words become unnecessary, and though Pat's mother hadn't been told her husband had died she also 'knew'. Pat, who lives on the Isle of Wight, telephoned me after she had heard a local radio phone-in in which I had been talking about telepathic bonds :

'My dad had senile dementia and also suffered with his chest as he'd been a miner. He was admitted to hospital for treatment. My mum was heartbroken. She was in Staffordshire and spent Christmas Day alone. She and my dad were never apart. Not long after, Mum was also taken into hospital with a bad chest. When I visited her she was in a bad way, very breathless and could hardly talk.

'I went to see Dad in his hospital and he was getting along well, so I didn't tell him how ill Mum was. I needed to get back to the children, but I stayed till Mum was on the mend.

'I promised, "I'll come back on Monday," but Mum insisted, "No, go back to your family. I'm doing fine."

'And she was better, or I would not have left her. The next morning the news came that Dad had suddenly died, and two hours later I heard that Mum was gone as well, though she hadn't been told about Dad.

'Before Mum was taken ill she had been convinced, "If anything happens to your dad, I won't last five minutes."

'I was upset because I thought she meant she'd commit suicide. My mum was very unhappy if she was apart from Dad, and couldn't bear to think of him going into a home if anything ever happened to her. Dad would never have managed without Mum. He relied on her for everything. Now I understood. They just had to be together, even in death.'

Pauline, an experienced nurse from Bristol, did not find this experience strange. She had seen patients turn their face to the wall and will themselves to die. One old lady she got to know while visiting her own sick mother, had been totally abandoned by her family, and although she was not terminally ill, died one morning, to the surprise of the doctors. But as Pauline remarked, "What did the old lady have to live for?"

What is remarkable is that Pat's mother sensed that her husband was gone and decided to follow him.

A very frequent and powerful intuitive link is between a

child and his or her grandparents, and from my own research
the link is as close with grandfathers as grandmothers. David
is a doctor who lives in Cambridge, USA, 76 miles from his
grand-daughter, two and a half year-old Marissa, his son
Daniel and his daughter-in-law Lauren. David responded to
an *Unsolved Mysteries* television programme that featured my
book on maternal intuition:

'I was very close to my two boys and first grandchild. The
incident happened on 23 March 1994. We'd had a terrible
winter so there hadn't been much travelling. I hadn't seen my
grand-daughter for a while. At 11 o'clock I was aware that I
should see my grand-daughter before something happened
to stop me seeing her. I felt bothered. My daughter-in-law
was due to have a baby within a month, but it wasn't that.

'I was shopping for a fridge and waiting for the manager to
do a deal. But at 1 p.m. I felt uncomfortable, that I had to go
and see my grand-daughter. The feeling got stronger and
stronger till the pain became exquisite. I finally abandoned
the shopping and drove fast the 76 miles. When I reached the
house at four, they were gone. The dog was in the back of the
house and the window was partly open so I knew Lauren
hadn't gone to have the baby. At that point my son came roar-
ing up in his car an hour ahead and said, "I can't stop.
Marissa's had an accident."

'Before long Marissa and her mother arrived home.
Marissa was very distressed. I got her mother to hold her
while I examined her. Marissa had a haemorrhage in her
palate and a loose tooth. Lauren was frantic as the doctor's
examination had been very poor and Marissa was still hurt
and in pain. She had stumbled on the kerb. I was able to
reassure Marissa and her mother and sort the problem out.
Now I understand why Marissa had needed me.

'When I got home, my wife said, "I've got something I want
you to watch." It was the *Unsolved Mysteries* segment about
maternal intuition she had taped. I was amazed as the programme mirrored my own experience with Marissa.'

When a relation is dying, it seems that he or she can communicate telepathically with a family member to whom they
are particularly bonded. This experience can happen over
many miles, and sometimes the dying person actually appears

to say goodbye. Russell Graves, from Massachusetts, shared his beloved grandfather's last moments. Russell believes that he had always been especially close to his grandfather, after whom he was named. Russell was working as an electrician for a power company:

'At 7 a.m. one morning I had the most terrible, sharp pain in my chest just like a heart attack. My grandad was perfectly healthy and had never had trouble with his heart. But I knew something was wrong with my grandfather, and went to my boss and told him I might need emergency leave. I tried to phone my parents' house but there was no answer, and my grandmother's phone was continually busy.

'Grandad lived just outside New York City and I was 100 miles away. I decided that I was being irrational and went back to work, but still felt very distressed. An hour or two later my landlord telephoned me and told me he was very sorry to say a message had come for me to say my grandfather had died of a heart attack. My grandfather had died at the time I had the terrible chest pains.

'I drove straight to my parents' home and thought it was all a mistake or a bad joke. My grandfather was there, but then I realised it was not he, but his brother, who resembles him closely, sitting in grandfather's chair. The fact I had known haunts me, and I wonder could I have done anything if I had acted at once? But how could I, as I shared his dying moments?

'All I have to remember my grandfather by is his clock'.

As with other telepathic experiences of the urgent kind, Russell acted out of character by telling his boss he might need emergency leave, before official channels had informed him of his grandfather's death.

In all family relationships these incidents occur, sometimes where a bond is particularly strong between two members, sometimes where parents may separately link into a child's distress, and the only explanation would seem to be that the link of love is powerful enough to use channels that aren't open to conscious manipulation. I have selected just a few out of many accounts I have received – most families have a story to tell somewhere in the family history. It may be that reading these triggers off some distant memory from your past. If so I would love to hear about it for it is only by collecting such experiences and reporting them that this very special power can be acknowledged openly as one many of us do possess.

John phoned me during a West Country radio phone-in. He told me that one Friday night he had gone to meet a friend at a pub for a drink while his wife had gone dancing with some of her friends:

'Throughout the evening I became increasingly worried that something awful had happened to our daughter Jenni, and I could not concentrate on or join in the banter and laughter. Unusually I made an excuse to leave early. As I walked out of the door I saw my wife coming across the car park towards me. She, too, had had dreadful feelings all evening and knew she must come and find me.

'It may seem strange now, but so strong were these emotions that we said that if we could not contact Jenni by phone at home we would go straight to the local hospital. Our daughter was not at home. She was in intensive care after a car crash that had occurred at the time we had both started to feel the fear.'

Often because of the dramatic nature of these experiences they may all seem to refer to doom and disaster. Yet it is natural that in times of distress we should call to our loved ones. John's experience had the positive result that he and his wife were able to go quickly to the hospital, and were able to react calmly because they had experienced the fears in advance. Jenni did recover, so the story has a happy ending.

It is not only the maternal link that works in reverse. Bill, who lives in Swindon, was a careful driver, but one evening his grown-up daughter sensed that he was in danger:

'One evening, while I was living in Oxford, I went out in the car. My grown-up daughter Alison, who is married, phoned my son's house to see if I was all right. He said I was. But Alison was still worried. A few minutes later, however, my son had a phone call to say I had been in a car crash. It was so bad that I had to be cut out of the vehicle.

'Later I asked Alison why she had phoned her brother, and she said she had felt something dreadful had happened to me'.

It is, however, possible to tune into happy family events, although even those are not guaranteed pain-free. Pam's younger sister Tanya was seven months pregnant. Pam suddenly had the most dreadful stomach pains:

'The pains became so bad I thought it was appendicitis, and so I called the GP, who sent me to hospital. However, the hospital doctor could find nothing wrong with me. The pains stopped quite suddenly. I later discovered that my sister had gone into very early labour at the other end of the country, and had given birth at the time my pains ceased.'

Although I have been researching psychic experiences for several years, I am still disappointed by the lack of father/ child experiences. Relatively few fathers have contributed similar stories, and on a whole there are even less cases of the routine telepathic contact that is so common between mothers and small children. I can only speculate that men still do not have the opportunity for the close everyday contact with their children. Experiences between boys and grandfathers are more usual, suggesting that an older man may have more time with the child, and perhaps is less motivated to spend that time in activity.

As a society, we still do not make it easy to discuss psychic experience, so it may be easier for women to come forward. In the early days of my research I wondered whether I was reaching a male audience, but over the years I have broadcast at different times of the day and received experiences from men on ghosts and premonitions, though more usually of people they do not know. I am reluctant to accept that the maternal bond is naturally stronger than the paternal, although this is one explanation, and wonder how men can get greater access to their children, and if they want it.

Barry, from Bolton, saw me on *This Morning*, an independent network chat show with Richard Madeley and Judy Finnegan, and he does have this routine telepathic link with his daughter:

'My young daughter Jennifer has the ability to pick up my thoughts. On one occasion, I was thinking about the three years of my childhood spent in Australia, and in particular a place called Lunar Park, which is a fun-fair near Sydney Harbour.

'Suddenly Jennifer said, "Can I go there?"
"Where?" I said.
"To that fun-fair," Jennifer replied.

'One night, it was 7 p.m. and I was considering whether to go to the college library to get a book and a few papers I wanted. I don't normally go to college in the evenings. However, I suddenly made up my mind it would be a good idea, and was about to tell my wife Lorraine what I had decided when Jennifer asked, "Can I come to college with you?"

Barry himself had psychic experiences as a child, and even now has vivid premonitions. This has perhaps helped him to recognise and acknowledge this bond with Jennifer.

Finally, remember, if you decide to stray from the straight and narrow, the most unlikely family member can tune into you, or worse still be drawn to your hiding place like a homing pigeon and blow the whistle. Pat, who comes from Yorkshire, recounted what seems to be the most unlikely chain of Chinese whispers. Such coincidences seem to imply that life isn't as random as some of us would like to think:

'My nephew Paul was to be married, a big society wedding that was cancelled at the last minute with no explanations given. I could not have cared less, but the children insisted, "Go on, mum, get on your broomstick and find out why".

'Soon after we went to France on holiday. I had five adolescents with me to feed, and we made for Camp Drammont. It was full, and so we went to a camp at Antheer Var. That also was very full, and while we were having supper two English children, David and Sarah, came to me and said, "Granny says she is very tired as she has driven from Le Touquet, and she says we must find an English family and stay with them until she wakes up."

'I fed David and Sarah for two days until Granny surfaced. I asked Sarah why she was with Granny, and received the reply, "Daddy has run away from Mummy with his friend Uncle Paul, and they have gone to Chamonix instead of Uncle Paul getting married."

'Of course my family hooted, "Good old mum".

'Martin, Paul's friend, is now married. At his wedding Sarah dashed up to us and blurted it all out. Everyone realised I knew about Paul's adventures.'

Is that psychic? I include it to suggest that the boundaries are very blurred between what sceptics would call a coincidence – Jung uses the term 'synchronicity' or 'meaningful coincidence' – and what might be called 'telepathic signals'. I don't believe there is a gigantic board in the sky on which people are moved like pawns to a certain place at a certain time, and yet the odds against Pat's experience occurring were very great.

We are sometimes instinctively and unconsciously drawn to a particular place at a particular time for apparently no reason. This is sometimes the way birthparents and the children they lost are reunited. Stories like Pat's are intriguing – the family web is very complex, and science does not have the tools to deal with such human complexity.

# 4

---

# FAMILIES AND PREMONITIONS

W hy do most premonitions refer to family events rather than international disasters? It may be that just as the mother and other family members have an automatic radar to link into danger to a loved one as it is happening, so too can we link into a peril that has not yet occurred. How a family member tunes into the future is not understood by scientists or philosophers. Perhaps time is circular, or family bonds so strong that in crisis they can operate outside the bounds of time and space.

Glen, who lives in Florida, told me how his wife's premonition saved their infant's life:

'We were living in Warren in Michigan. One late afternoon in November 1952 I put our two-month old baby in the bed as I had done many times. Suddenly my wife knew she had to move the baby urgently and put him in his crib. She had no idea why. Three minutes later our house was struck by lightning and the ceiling fell in the bedroom and living room. We and the baby were in the only safe place in the house where the ceilings did not come down.

'Had my wife not moved the baby at that moment, he would have been killed. The lightning burned the pillows on the bed where the baby had been lying and seared right through the bed. I had no inkling of danger and when I asked my wife later why she had moved the baby she said she just knew she had to as he was in mortal danger on the bed. We still have the photos of the devastation caused to our house by the storm.'

This spontaneous predictive ability seems to me very different from deliberately trying to tell the future. The division is crucial – between a well-documented, need-driven ability, and attempts to make money by forecasting other people's fortunes. Many clairvoyants are honest and honourable and would not dream of foretelling doom. But there is a wide gulf between intuitively picking up issues from a person's past, and then going on to claim the power to determine the client's future. Many people do contact me in great distress because a fortune teller or tarot reader has predicted disaster for the person concerned or a family member. No one can do this, and you should not give such worthless advice a moment's thought, much less part with your money to consult that particular clairvoyant again.

Premonitions that happen naturally are very different and on occasions, as for Glenn's son, can be lifesavers if we listen to the warning.

However, this ability to see into the future of loved ones is not purely a maternal ability. David Collyer, a Birmingham vicar and radio presenter, had his premonition of family danger the night before the incident actually took place:

'I had a dream in which a car came out of a field and smashed into our family car. I told my wife, but I was not worried as I was not anticipating any travel that day.

'However, unexpectedly I was asked to make a journey and we set off in the car. I came to a spot and recognised it from my dream. I told my wife and she reassured me that there were no signs of an accident, and indeed there was not even any other traffic.

'I told her that in my dream the car had come out of a field, for the place was the one I had seen the night before. As I looked, a car did come hurtling out of the field. I swerved into the ditch and the family was saved. I believe this was because I was alerted.'

David was fairly certain his dream referred to an event that would happen quickly, and trusted his forewarning. Where do premonitions originate – from an outside source, God or a guardian angel, or from within our own deep intuitive abilities that allows us access to information beyond the conscious sphere? I prefer the latter explanation, but we really do not know. Perhaps it is significant that the majority of premonitions do come while we are asleep. It may be that premonitions occur more easily during dreams because that is the time our conscious barriers are at their lowest, and so information from a normally inaccessible source can reach us.

Sceptics argue that we dream of disaster many times and nothing happens. That is so, and given the number of air crash dreams, it is more than likely that someone somewhere has predicted them. However the difference, as with genuine premonition, especially one involving the family, is the intensity of the dream or vision. In the first chapter I told how Jennifer Moss's mother was desperate to prevent the couple at the Spanish hotel from catching a particular plane. Hers was not a dream, but the principle is the same. What is more Jennifer's mother was not prone to begging people not to travel.

Elise, from Dallas, Texas, is convinced that by listening to her dream she saved her mother's life:

'I called my mother very early one morning to warn her not to go shopping to the sales with her friend later that morning because something bad would happen. I'd dreamed I saw her friend's car wrecked very badly and my mother was in it. In the dream they were both killed and I knew it would happen almost as soon as they set out. Mom asked me if I'd been drinking (I never touch alcohol). I cried and made her promise me she'd wait until the next day to go to the sales. She agreed but said she thought I was mad.

'That morning at 9.10, her friend went on alone. A truck jumped a red light three blocks away from Mom's house and hit the car. Her friend was killed instantly. The truck hit the passenger side where my mom would have been sitting. Mom phoned me to ask me how I'd known, but I couldn't explain.'

We need no special psychic powers to have such an experience, just trust in our own powerful protective senses. I was a slow psychic developer. It took until Bill, my fifth child, was almost five to trust my early warning system. Bill was at the limpet stage. If I went out in the car, shopping or to ferry one of the older children, Bill came too. One evening in March 1993, I had to take Jade to the local town of Freshwater, about two miles distant. Bill trotted to the door as usual with his coat, but I suddenly and urgently knew he must not come. I am not sure exactly what I said, something like, "You can't come because the car will go too fast," which did not make a great deal of sense.

'More surprisingly Bill said, "All right, Mummy, I'll stay."

'When we reached the outskirts of Freshwater, there was a diversion and the buses were using the narrow back lanes. A bus came towards me too fast in the middle of the road. I braked to let it past, skidded and the car ended up on top of some marker posts about 2 ft. 6 high. It was so remarkable that one or two of the locals came to take photos. Had the car wheels moved an inch further the car would have tipped over. One of the posts had gone through the suspension and had Bill been in the back seat he would have been badly hurt.'

I do not claim any special psychic powers and, indeed, do not believe that inherited paranormal gifts account for psychic families, even where experiences are more frequent. Others would disagree.

Like mine, all premonitions are not as detailed as Elise's, and may involve a growing sense of unease and panic rather than specific images. The problem is trusting these instincts. We may take evasive action, especially when our children are involved, and never know whether we over-reacted.

Carol who lives in California, was not at all an anxious mother. However, she is confident that she did save her son's life by listening to a premonition of unspecified danger:

'In 1977, when my son was 14, I was working the second shift. My elder daughter was caring for my son at home. I was suddenly overshadowed by a terrible fear and feeling that I had to get my son away that weekend until I knew it was safe to return, and there was no time to waste.

'The feeling of imminent danger was so strong I quit my job and gave the house and car to my daughter, whom I knew was not involved in the danger and did not wish to come. I took my son to Santa Barbara, where we stayed in a spiritual community. While we were there I felt totally protected and knew the danger had not followed us. However, I was still aware that it was not yet safe to take my son home.

'After two weeks, I felt the peril had passed. My best friend came to fetch us and she took me to my mom's house. To my amazement the television was on, most unusual for my parents who did not watch daytime TV. An announcement was made that the police had just captured a serial killer in Angel Street near where I live. He was taking away blonde-haired boys from the streets and murdering them. My son then admitted that, unknown to me, while I had been at work, he had been out in the evenings riding his bike round the streets, including Angel Street. He was finely built and very good-looking.'

Sally, from Berkshire, also told me how she believes that the feeling of impending disaster she and her mother shared may have prompted them to pray at the crucial moment her brother was involved in a potentially fatal crash. Because of this, Sally is convinced her brother's life was spared:

'When I was 13 my mum worked shifts at the local hospital. One morning I woke up with the terrible feeling she was going to die. I didn't want to upset my mother by telling her, but I insisted I went to work with her. As the day progressed I felt increasingly anxious. Mum, too, had a growing sensation that something dreadful was going to happen. She did not say anything to me as *she* did not want to upset *me*. However, she did tell two friends at work about her fear. On the way home in the car Mum suddenly said, "Shall we stop at a church and say a prayer?"

'I agreed, and was incredibly relieved. Unknown to us, while we were praying my older brother Anthony was involved in a car accident. Soon after we got home there was a knock at the door. Mum said, "Oh God, something has happened to Anthony!"

'It was a friend of Anthony's who had called to break the news that the car in which Anthony had been travelling had been going too fast round a bend on a country road and had hit a tree. The police said all the occupants of the car should have been killed. Amazingly, Anthony and his friends walked away unhurt. I am convinced we picked up the danger although we did not understand it, and so were led to pray at the time when Anthony needed help most.'

Was this another case of the power of prayer and family love saving lives? Sally had lost her father not long before, so it would have been easy for Sally and her mother to dismiss their panic as natural anxiety and a reaction to bereavement. But the feeling was so strong both Sally and her mother responded to the unknown need.

If we do have the opportunity to save a beloved child or parent's life, for many premonitions do centre around this integral bond, what greater reward can there be? However, as I have said many times in my books, some mothers and fathers who are equally loving, caring parents never get a chance or warning. I do not know why this should be, and I am aware that stories of parents who do get warnings can particularly distress those who lose children through cot deaths or accident. For that reason I do worry about including such accounts.

However, I do include cases where a life is saved as well as those where it is not, because the message to trust your intuitions, whether on a life and death or everyday basis, is vital.

Not all premonitions end happily, especially if there is no time-scale. I would be selling you short if I tidied this chapter and came up with total reassurance. Why then are we told of a disaster or have a sense of foreboding concerning a family member that we cannot prevent either because there are no details or the time scale is not clear? Even if we do not know the what and the why, a premonition can enable us to be there for a beloved relative, to offer love and support. If we feel someone close needs us then we should go to them, and if they do not want us around then at least we have shown our love and can beat a hasty retreat. But usually, a sign of affection and support is welcomed, even if not fully understood.

Fathers can, as I have said, have strong intuitive bonds with their children. When they do occur they suggest the undeveloped capacity of men to use their intuitions.

Lesley Westrum from Wisconsin was fast asleep when her

Dad turned up out of the blue in the middle of the night with her mum and younger brother. Lesley explained:

'I went downstairs in the middle of the night for a drink and tripped over something. That something was my brother's legs. He was lying on our living room floor in a sleeping bag, which you don't expect when you live several hundred miles from your family. He woke up and that woke my parents, who sat up to tell me they'd slipped in quietly so as not to disturb me.

'My son's birthday was the next day, and they told me some lame story about how they hadn't got his birthday present to the post in time so they brought it in person. It sounded suspicious to me. But it was a nice visit.

'I was pregnant and two weeks later I went into labour. I rang my mom to tell her she'd be a grandma and they decided to come up for the occasion. As usual I had a long labour.

'When the baby was born she was perfect, instantly beautiful, tiny and perfectly formed, none of the usual premature breathing problems – I got to nurse her on the delivery table. She looked different from my other babies before or since. In her eyes was a wisdom as if she knew everything. She was a wise old spirit in a baby's body. Seven hours later she died.

'Later my dad told me about the night he'd arrived out of the blue. He'd known something was wrong and he'd packed Mama and my brother and driven across country to see if there was anything he could do. On seeing me he realised I was in no danger but that it was the baby. He knew there was nothing he could do and so he kept his own counsel rather than worry me.'

So what was the point of her Dad's premonition? The unexpected visit was a tangible demonstration of the deep love within the family, which gave Lesley strength to face the tragedy ahead. Life can be cruel, and sometimes all we are left with is a sense that we are loved and that there must be some deeper meaning to tragedy, even if we cannot apprehend it.

Like many mothers, Linda Peck, of Tasmania, Australia, knew the sex of her unborn child, even though doctors insisted otherwise. She lost her child, who was born only 18 weeks into the pregnancy, and knew from early on that things would not go well. Her premonition enabled her to stop her husband having a vasectomy and enabled her to value the short time she did have with her unborn child.

Linda's is not a sad story. She believes she was very close to her infant and shared a deep bond of love. She told me:

'I am a 33-year-old mother of three, but it is the story of the infant I lost after 18 weeks of pregnancy that I should like to share. It started with me feeling very ill. I went to my GP and asked him for a pregnancy test. I already had a baby three months old but I knew I was going to have another baby. The doctor did not wish me to have any more children but I did the test. I was pregnant and glad about it. I loved this baby. I knew it was a girl, I had not had any test to find out. I just knew. I knitted and crocheted for a baby girl.

'I began to get very worried, but I did not know why. My husband Ray was to have a vasectomy on the Tuesday before I was to have my 18-week scan. I asked him to cancel it, as I was very concerned about the baby. But I still couldn't tell why. I had had a scan at six weeks and the baby was fine and we had heard the baby's heartbeat at about 14 to15 weeks.

'As the day of the scan got closer, my fears got stronger. I told Ray I didn't want to go for the scan but still did not know or could not say why. Ray, knowing me the way he does, realised that I did not worry for no good reason. So he was concerned, but more for me.

'On Friday, Ray went with me for the scan. Thank God Ray was there as the doctor told me what I did not wish to hear. Our baby had died. I think I knew, but did not want to admit it. But there was still more. After the birth, which had to be induced five days later, we were told the baby had been a boy. I knew the nurses were wrong, but said nothing. I was too upset. But 24 hours later the nurses apologised and said my baby had been a girl. I have never felt so close to a baby as I did with Gabrielle, the name we gave our very little baby girl. She was only 90g.'

Judi, whom I met in Los Angeles, described in Chapter 2 how a telepathic link saved her son, Corey. Yet a few years earlier she had an unspecified premonition of danger and loss concerning her elder son Craig, but was unable to save him. However, Judi believes that the warning did give her a chance to express her love to her child and to say goodbye:

'My husband, my son Corey and I moved to Massachusetts in 1985, only living there for six weeks before moving back to Indiana. We didn't like it out there. My eldest son, Craig, was a military policeman in the US Army, stationed at Fort Dix in New Jersey. As my birthday neared, my husband asked me what I wanted. I told him the only thing I wanted for my birthday was to see Craig. We couldn't drive to New Jersey on my birthday, but made arrangements to go down a week or so later. We spent a day with Craig, and as we were leaving I hugged him goodbye as I always do with my children.

'But for some reason, which I did not understand, I did not want to let go of him. I must have stood there for five minutes, hugging him, kissing him and telling him how much I loved him. He laughed it off, though he was pleased, saying he did not know what had got into his mom. I cried as we drove away, watching him standing there waving goodbye to us.

'Could I have known that in less than three weeks he would be gone? We took a lot of pictures that day and I even took a picture of his new stereo, which was the kind with several components on shelves in a standing cabinet with glass doors. He laughed at that too, and said that he didn't know why I wanted a picture of his stereo. I didn't know why either.

'About a week after returning to Indiana I awoke about 3.30 on Sunday morning, Memorial Day weekend. I felt sad and very troubled. I got up and went to the family room to sit. Because it was so unusual for me to get up in the middle of the night, my husband came to check on me. I told him I was fine and that he should go back to bed which he did. All I could think of was Craig. When my husband got up later that morning he told me I looked as if I had lost my best friend. Because I did not feel like talking to anyone, I went outside to work in my flower garden. Whenever I am troubled, I work with my flowers. But this day even my flowers did not make me feel better. I constantly thought of Craig and felt very sad.

'Around 11.30 that morning an Army captain came to our home and informed us that Craig had been killed the night before in a motorcycle accident. Although the accident occurred at 1 30 a.m., pronouncement of death was not made until Craig's body arrived at the mortuary at 3.30 a.m., the time I awoke. I have always thought Craig stayed with his body until he was pronounced dead and then he came to me. I have no way of knowing for sure.

'My brother, who is four years younger than me, has always been psychic, although he has tried to discourage it and didn't want it. I think he has finally succeeded because he no longer has psychic experiences. After Craig's accident, however, Craig would come to my brother. We received a lot of messages from Craig, and I treasure every one of them. One afternoon, probably a couple of weeks after Craig's death, I was alone at home and talking to Craig.

'I was feeling depressed and was telling Craig how much I missed him and how much I wished I knew he did not suffer pain after the accident. After a while I felt I would go crazy if I did not get out of the house for a while. I went to my parents' home. My brother had lived with my parents for several years and was there when I arrived. As I walked in the front door he said, "Oh, that's why".

'I asked him what he was talking about, and he told me Craig had been there and had shown him the accident. Craig had told him he should remember he was seeing the crash exactly as Craig had experienced it. In the vision, the motorcycle had two men on it. Craig had been passenger on the motorcycle which was being driven by another military policeman. My brother saw the motorcycle hit the back bumper of an automobile and flip over, throwing both men against a guard rail along the road. He told me that although he had shared the entire accident, he had viewed it from above as Craig was saying he had done. Then I knew that Craig had not suffered at all, that God had been merciful and removed Craig from his body before the impact.

'No one will ever know how greatly this has helped me to endure Craig's loss, how much it meant to hear Craig had not suffered. It has been almost ten years and I still talk to Craig a lot. I have often wondered if it was Craig who came to me when Corey had his accident and told me to pray for Corey. Maybe it is just my bond with Corey that saved him. I probably will never know, but I am certainly thankful for whatever it was.

'As for the picture I took of Craig's stereo, it came back to me with all Craig's possessions from the army. Because I had the picture, we knew how the stereo was supposed to be arranged in the cabinet. We probably would have had a devil of a job trying to figure it out without the picture. We still have the stereo in our living room and use it constantly.'

In Chapter 2, Sandra described how she felt an intense pain at the time her son Gifford was killed on his motorcycle, and so also 'knew' Gifford had not suffered.

Why should Judi be able to save Corey and not Craig, with whom she was equally bonded? Judi took comfort from the last loving meeting. However, some parents do not feel that a premonition helped. Indeed, in a few cases a premonition can cause unnecessary guilt. This is, in part, because so few people are comfortable giving a bereaved person the opportunity to explore all avenues. Guilt is a part of any grieving process. Where there is a paranormal element, professionals and friends may be dismissive and leave the grieving person with unresolved conflicts.

Researchers often try to verify premonitions without considering the human aspect, and I am aware that I don't have any easy answers. Anne, who lives in Staffordshire, lives with the guilt that had she told someone of her premonition her son might have been saved. She telephoned me and I found that, ten years later, she was suffering many problems related to her son's death, including agoraphobia. From what she told me she has been given tranquillisers and anti-depressants for years, but no practical help or support:

'I dreamed that my youngest son, David, aged 14, had been in an accident. He was lying in the road with his bike close by. I woke up screaming and with tears falling down my face. I ran into my son's room and found him fast asleep.

'I went back to bed, hoping to forget it. But I could not sleep and the horrible experience went round and round in my mind as it was so real. I could not get it out of my mind despite telling myself it was only a dream.

'I didn't tell anyone because I thought they would say I was stupid. However, this dream became reality. Two weeks later, my 14-year-old son was killed as he was coming home with his pal, exactly the way I had dreamed it would happen.

'I'm still absolutely devastated, though it's been ten years. I still cannot accept David is gone and I cry every day. My son did not stand a chance. The drunken driver ran off after the accident and left my son dying in the road along with his pal.

'The week following David's death, I had an experience of him coming to me as I lay in bed. First of all it was like a white/ grey mist. Then David appeared. I wanted desperately to hold on to him. It was so peaceful but then I reached out to touch him and he disappeared. Since then there has been nothing. The experience did not heal my heartbreak. I feel I am broken. It has really destroyed me, and the dream I had haunts me. I believe had I told David or someone, it may not have happened. So I am also feeling guilty. The driver eventually came to court and got 240 hours' community service. I am the one doing the life sentence.'

How could I advise Anne, except to encourage her to insist she got the medical help she was entitled to, and to assure her that there was no way she was to blame for her son's death. Medical practitioners who pontificate that it is wrong to pro-long grief by recognising and bringing into the open paranormal factors that may have been involved, should talk to Anne, who has carried her secret burden for ten years.

However, not all premonitions foretell disaster. Some can give hope that all will be well. Pamela's message came in the form of a dream. When Pamela was eight, her father became very ill:

'I prayed to Our Lady. She showed me snow covered steps leading to an altar set in a bay. I tried to follow, but my steps scuffed the snow. Ahead was my father and Our Lady. She stopped to show me the steps of his life ahead of him. She was so beautiful. My father lived till I was 22. We moved to the place where he died, with the beautiful bay, when I was 16.'

The vision gave Pamela great comfort at a time when she was afraid her father would die. At the time of the dream they did not live near the sea.

Science and physiology can offer no channels for such

communication. We have to rely on the experiences of those who have felt such a call. Louise, who lives in Macclesfield, was 30 weeks pregnant when a scan first revealed that her unborn infant had a brain cyst. It was a sign from the baby in the womb that gave her the confidence to go against the advice of doctors.

The consultant wanted to do a Caesarean at 30 weeks, as he was worried the brain cyst would be growing rapidly and would destroy the brain. The consultant told Louise that an adult with such a brain cyst would probably be dead or severely mentally and physically disabled. Louise was given the weekend to decide what to do, and was considering going ahead with the Caesarean despite her fears that the baby might not survive.

However, when her mind was almost made up not to go ahead with the pregnancy the baby began kicking very vigorously, which he had not done before. He even kicked things off her stomach, and was so active he could not be ignored. It seemed to Louise as though the baby was telling her to hold on and give him a chance. From that moment Louise bonded with the baby and felt a protective love. As a result of this prediction from within her womb that all would be well, Louise decided against the operation.

Although her husband Tony felt it better to clear the nursery of toys and baby clothes as the prognosis on the baby was so bad, Louise kept one rattle, which she hid in the drawer of her bedside cabinet. The baby, whom Louise's daughter had called Jack the weekend he started kicking, was induced at 37 weeks. When Jack was born, Louise held him close. He opened his eyes and looked into hers and she knew that Jack would survive and was a normal infant. A fortnight after his birth Jack was given a special scan. The consultant told Louise the good news, that the cyst wasn't spreading to the left side of his brain, which controls movement, speech and hearing, and that his brain was totally undamaged.'

Louise's premonition was based on pure instinct, for logic and medical expertise predicted that the baby would either die or be very severely damaged. We do not fully understand the nature of communication between mother and unborn child. There are those who would say that it was pure coincidence that Jack began to kick so much the weekend when his future was held in the balance. What is important is that Louise had the courage to go against the experts and give Jack the chance of life.

Some premonitions can be a way of rehearsing an event so that when it occurs in real life we are assured we will be safe and so do not panic. David, from Birmingham, recalls a premonition concerning his family that helped him through a terrifying situation:

'As a child during the last world war I lived in an isolated and small village in Gloucestershire with my grandmother, in a cottage at the bottom of a lane. My mother and father lived at the top of the lane. When I was nine or ten I had a terrifying dream that I have never forgotten. In the dream there was an earthquake which shook the village and people came running from their cottages and congregated at the top of the lane, including my mother, my father, my grandmother and myself. We ran for the woods that surrounded the village, and as we ran my grandmother cried out, "Oh, God, they will get us this time". Then I woke up.

'On the following night there was a terrible air raid. The German bombers tried to get to the aerodrome which was near us on the outskirts of Bristol. As it was one of the first heavy raids, we were not organised, and my grandmother and I sat under the stairs of her cottage in the light of a small oil lamp. Noise increased all around us from the aircraft overhead, and then bombs were dropped very near by and seemed to be coming towards us. Suddenly my grandmother said the words that she had uttered in my dream the previous night, "Oh God, they will get us this time", and I was not afraid any more because I knew that we had survived the night before.'

How can someone tell the difference between a premonition and normal anxiety, and not jump to conclusions that danger to loved ones is just around the corner? Am I not just increasing the pressures on already anxious parents, especially first-time ones?

If you feel, "I wonder whether I ought to check on my child", or are constantly feeling anxious, these are not premonitions but a sign that you need to talk about the underlying worries with someone helpful. Those nagging fears that keep family members awake at night, worrying about the well-being of those we love, are the other side of the coin of love, and anxiety is bound up with caring. If we don't care we don't love, and vice versa.

In contrast, trusting your instincts can actually lower your anxiety level, and if you do suddenly get the call of danger and you are wrong, at worst you will look a fool. Sometimes stories of other people's premonitions of danger to their children are a reminder to love our own, whatever age they may be and with all their imperfections and differences in lifestyle, and be glad they are alive and well.

# 5

# FAMILY GHOSTS

Most ghosts – a presence which retains the earthly form – are family members, loved and recognised by those who see them. Often they come bringing comfort and love at a time when we are feeling alone or neglected. Grand-mothers are by far the most common family ghost, and they usually come to see a grandchild who is unhappy or having problems. Grandparents have a relationship that is not as fraught as the direct parent/child one, and can mediate in family quarrels. The peacemaker role may continue after death.

Jane, who lives in Lincolnshire, wrote to me about 'an experience that happened when I was 16 years of age that convinced me that my granny is watching over me.

'I got into some trouble with my mum and I thought now my gran was dead I had no one to talk to. When Gran died, I was only eight years old and she was like a second mother to me. She looked after me when I was a baby. We had a bond that was not broken even by her death. I do believe that when I have a problem that I can tell no one else, she is still there. I can feel her. We have never spoken to each other directly but it makes me feel better knowing she is there for me.

'Before my gran died I knew she had come into the room by

the lovely perfume which she always wore. Now I feel her presence when I am upset or worried.

'The problem I had with my mum was the usual teenage one of growing up, rows etc. It was a Sunday in October and I went with my other grandma to the graveyard to visit my gran's and my grandmother's mother's grave. When we left the graveyard I felt very lonely. For the first time since Gran had died I smelled her perfume very strongly and I heard her call my name. I turned round and saw my grandma standing there in the road just smiling at me. I felt warm and comforted by her, and knew she was telling me that she was there and would never leave me.

'I only told my mum some weeks after the event, but I don't think she believed me. It's not frightening to see a loved one. It's a nice experience of warmth, love and a sense of knowing what will happen after you die'.

However, it is very easy to doubt that the contact was authentic. Some people are happy just to accept the experiences, but others may worry that they are creating a scenario, especially if those they tell are sceptical. June, from Wiltshire, recalled that when her grandmother died she could still sense her around and even heard her sending loving messages in her head:

'Gran told me one day, "I'm all right now, love."

'But I had doubts that I was inventing the whole thing. So I asked Gran, "If you really are talking to me, tell me where my lost ring is".

'I'd lost my engagement ring, which was valuable as well as precious, a few days before, and I had turned the house upside down to find it.

'"It's in the washing machine, stuck in the rubber hose," Gran told me.

'And sure enough the ring was there, though I have no idea how it got into the hose.'

Jennifer, a nurse from Wales, also has a story about her mother that seems inexplicable except in terms of paranormal contact. She is certain her four-year-old twins, John and James, see their late grandmother regularly, and that a dream at their conception began the link:

'The twins have chatted over the past two years, since they

could talk properly, in fact, about the Blue Lady, whom they first saw in their small bedroom, and have seen since on numerous occasions. She wears blue, smiles and has dark hair. There is a lovely gold light round her and she has a white horse. At first we thought the children were having a vision of the Virgin Mary.

'Then they described the lady as having no hair and blood coming from her mouth. My mother had myeloid leukaemia diagnosed when I was eight weeks pregnant with the boys and died when I was six months pregnant.

'The strange dream I had around the point of the twins' conception may or may not be contributory to their *in utero* memory banks and/or their psychic senses.

'I dreamed of a single white horse bathed in a golden light, carrying two golden-haired young boys. Sure enough, an early scan at eight weeks revealed two foetuses. The other part of my dream revealed my mother's funeral, six months before it took place. I was unaware of her diagnosis or illness at the time of the dream.

'Moira, my mother, adored the colour blue and had dark hair. She suffered hair loss and oral haemorrhage during the last weeks of her life. This latter vision was especially seen by John.'

Jennifer is now convinced that her mother is with the boys and cares for them. Her appearance with the blood and hair loss did not worry the children. Was Jennifer's mother trying to let her know in an unmistakable way it really was her?

Children have an amazing knack of picking up seemingly irrelevant detail in their experiences with their grandmothers, that confirms to the adults that the experience was more than childish fantasy. It may be easier for young children to make contact because they don't have the same barriers of logic or disbelief. Gran is still Gran whether she has died or just popped round the corner to do the shopping.

Since her death, George's late wife Celia has made contact with several family members. But it is with her granddaughter Jane that the closest bonds have remained. George, who lives in Nuneaton, is entirely happy about this:

'My three-year-old grand-daughter Jane can see my late

wife. A few weeks ago she was out in my garden. We could hear her talking and saying, " Granny, Granny" and a whole lot of conversation in between.

'When she came in she pointed to my wife's photo three times, saying quite spontaneously, "That's Granny in the garden".

'When she got home her mother remarked, "I heard you talking to Granny."

"Oh, yes," replied Jane, "Granny told me she wasn't wearing her usual dress today. Her new one is purple. That's God's colour".

'The strange thing was the same night, my daughter-in-law, on holiday in Florida, dreamed she was in the garden with Celia but she could not see her. Then she saw a small purple waterfall and my wife was there, dressed in purple too.'

This was not the first contact Jane had had with her granny. George explained:

'I decided to have Celia buried in a pink dress and pink shoes, but of course my grand-daughter did not see her and was not told about the choice of clothes. One Sunday, not long after, Jane started waving and smiling. Her mother asked who she was waving to, and Jane replied, "Granny went by in the sky."

'Her mother questioned what Granny was wearing, and Jane said her pink dress and shoes. Jane often says she plays outside with Granny, and when she was told on one occasion to come in out of the rain, turned and said, "Hurry up, Granny, or you will get wet too".'

George himself has had contact with his wife, and believes she foresaw her own death:

'Celia was a firm believer in the after-life and read the teacups. She was always right. All her life she would not say goodbye to anyone. But during the last week of her life, when the family left she said goodbye to them, and waited until they got to the end of the street to shout goodbye again.

'I have twin sons. Shortly before my wife's unexpected death, one dreamed of sitting round the table discussing a family funeral. Celia had the same dream the same night. She said, "I was there but I could not see myself. I hope I am not going to die."

'Then the other twin dreamed of a big black raven at the same time which we took to be a bad sign.

'When the doctor came for Celia's routine monthly visit she said to my wife, "See you next month as usual". My wife replied, "Doctor, I don't think I will see you next month," and a few days afterwards she died suddenly in my arms from a heart attack.

'Over the weekend the family cleared up after the funeral, when the relatives had gone. On our fiftieth wedding anniversary, my grandson had a big picture taken of my wife and myself, two foot square. It hung on the wall behind our chairs so when visitors came they could see it.

'Now I asked one of the children to move the picture to the wall in front of my chair so I could still see Celia.

'Ten days after her death I went to a spiritualist circle. A young girl at the circle told me that my wife was saying that I had moved her picture and would I please put it back so that she could look down on me again. The young medium also spoke about the chronic pains Celia had had in her left arm. She also mentioned how when my wife stretched up to check that the windows were locked as we made the supper the night before she died, I told Celia she was not supposed to do that.

'I had scolded my wife and Celia had snapped at me and said, "Well I won't do it again," and of course she did not, as she died at 6 a.m. the next morning.

'Celia got into a bit of a huff, but we kissed and cuddled before we went to sleep, which is a good job we did. She died with love between us. I was the last person she spoke to. The spiritualist told me all this, even about the pain my wife had down the middle of her chest immediately before she collapsed. I had got up at 6 a.m. and Celia had come in, rubbing the middle of her chest, saying she had an awful pain, which was when she died.'

Sonia also lost her husband suddenly, but at first found the contact frightening:

'My husband had died four years previously and I was going through a very worrying time. I felt desperate. I went to bed as usual one night, but suddenly felt wide awake. I half sat up, and yet at the same time I knew I was still flat on the bed. I

felt as if I was two people, one awake and the other
asleep.

'Then my husband was in bed with me. Although I never
saw him, I could feel his body close to mine, warm as it always
was in life. He put his arms round me and held me tightly. He
did not speak, nor did I. I don't know how long the
experience lasted, but during this time the room was
bright.

'Then I looked up and the room was in darkness, and I was
alone and terribly frightened that I was going mad. This
experience happened five times on different nights, and each
time I felt my husband getting stronger and trying desperately to contact me. But I was so frightened I went to my
doctor. He told me I wasn't going mad, but that it was my subconscious playing tricks and he put me on tranquillisers.

'One day walking home from work I had a feeling of peace
and calm come over me and I knew everything would be all
right, and from then on it was. I am now certain there is
another world and I have nothing to fear when I die. In fact, it
may be quite exciting.'

The loss of a partner early in life can be especially devastating. Susan explained:

'My husband died when he was only 32, leaving me to
bring up three young daughters, whom I made my life, and I
enjoyed working hard for them. We have always been a close
and loving family.

'Three years after my husband died, I remember late one
evening the moon was shining very brightly. I looked out of a
window and saw my husband quite clearly standing in the
garden, looking towards the house. Then after a few
moments the vision faded. No traumatic events led up to this
incident, but the children were asleep and I was feeling very
lonely. The appearance of my husband made me realise he
was still with me.'

Such experiences are not surprising between partners who
have shared many important moments, and perhaps many
years of marriage. Such visitations can be immensely comforting to the bereaved partner. I had assumed that the official
religious position would discourage such encounters. However, Canon Geoffrey Hunter, vicar of Heslington in

Yorkshire, explained that the Church of England does not have a definite position on the bereaved seeing dead relatives:

'There have been a number of reports on bereavement brought out by particular groups or dioceses.

'Undoubtedly people do believe they have been aware of the presence of a deceased member of the family. What percentage of people have such experiences isn't known, but I suspect it is far higher than is often guessed at. Some people may not report such an incident because they feel it is not significant and is part of the shock of being bereaved. Others feel anxious not to say anything in case they are regarded as having gone off their head. But the numbers are neither here nor there.

'What is important is what people do with the experience. Theologically it is not a problem. It is the way human beings function. When you have such an experience you can admit to yourself that you are distressed, and it can be part of the working your way through the grieving process. So it is constructive rather than destructive. Outsiders are often unwilling to talk about death, which can be very hurtful for the bereaved person. In theological circles, it has been considered in recent years whether we should adopt ministrations for the departed.

'In the Roman Catholic and High Anglican tradition there has always been the notion of the Requiem Eucharist for the departed, and for hundreds of years this practice has been held in suspicion by lower churches and evangelists. Now we are re-looking at this medieval church practice, that came about because of disasters such as the Black Death, and seeing it did serve some useful function. I would hope that the local priest would provide general support in time of bereavement, and such institutions as Cruse and the Samaritans can provide excellent help. Many parishes, including my own, do have groups for the bereaved. Seeing or sensing dead relatives is one of the factors that is dealt with in normal ministry and is part of the natural world in the human sense.

'I believe fervently in the communion of saints where the worlds of dead and living meet at the altar rail. If a man has lost his wife, I will encourage him to talk about his partner, recall her, and he can continue to celebrate his union with her at church. When widows go out of the church door after the service I say, "How is Robbie?" and his wife may go along to the grave and have a little chat with him and then come back and say, "I gave Robbie your best wishes."

'The communion of saints means all God's people, living or dead, and the cruellest thing we can do to a widow is to steer the conversation away from the dead person as if he never existed.'

Often children are forgotten in the grief when a brother or sister dies, and they may find it hard to make sense of the experience. They may fear that they, too, may die, or somehow caused the death by their own bad behaviour. Mandy, who lives in Staffordshire, was the eldest daughter of nine children, and like many eldest girls in a large family, perhaps developed a strong link with her siblings because she felt responsible for their welfare. Does this explain the bond she kept with her dead sister?

'My mother lost a beautiful baby girl. Her name was Lesley. She was nine months old when she died, and always so full of life. I will never forget the pain and grief on Mom's face. She nearly cried herself to death. Her eyes were red as though they were going to bleed.

'I was only nine years old. But I wondered then what happened to babies and people when they die. One night, months later, the family went to sleep and I was just going to sleep myself when I heard someone running around on the oilcloth in the baby's room, and it sounded just like a small child. The next morning I told my mom, but she thought I was making it up. Then my sister Maria came running in.

'"Mom, a little girl came into my room last night. She sat on my bed and stroked my hair. Then she disappeared."

'I was pleased because I knew I had heard a child, and the next day I asked my teacher, "Why are we born if we have to die?"

'She told me not to be silly.

'One night before Lesley died, my dad was late home and my mom was worried and went to see if she could find him. It was very quiet. I was sitting in an armchair and fell asleep.

The next thing I knew was the old clock on the mantelpiece chiming. I went to check the baby and went into the bedroom. A lady was bending over the cot. She was tucking the baby in. I wasn't frightened because she looked as if she belonged in that room. She had white wavy hair, very neat, and was dressed in her nightclothes and slippers.

'The woman turned round and smiled at me. She had the most lovely blue eyes. Then she was gone, just like a bubble.

'When my mum and dad came home I said, "My gran has been here," but Mom told me not to be stupid, as my nan was at home in bed asleep. I didn't mean that gran. I said Gran because the lady looked like my gran, only more old-fashioned, and I knew she had come to take care of the baby.

'Just after Christmas, when Lesley would have been a year old, a very black Christmas, the pram kept rocking by itself. Mom and Dad had gone out one night, and while they were away I heard a knocking upstairs. I turned the television off and sat listening. I was really scared. My brother came home and asked, "What's that noise upstairs?"

'It was Lesley's crib rocking. We went to look if Mom and Dad were coming home, as we were getting more and more frightened. Mom and Dad came home early, and as they walked through the door the rocking stopped. My brother and I didn't say anything as Mom was very strict about things like that. I used to think to myself often that the baby was still in the house.

'One morning I went upstairs to make the beds. I saw the pram rocking, and the bedroom door slammed shut and would not open. I called for my mom. She came upstairs and the door opened straight away. She thought I was playing games as there wasn't a lock on the door.'

Mandy had problems because her mother found it hard to accept Mandy's experiences of her lost sister. This caused Mandy, like many children in similar situations, pain and unnecessary guilt.

Where there is no guilt and where psychic experiences are accepted as a part of life, children can naturally find a way of making sense of the transition between death and life. Kath, from Manchester, is very open to spiritual and psychic experience, and helped her daughter to incorporate the vision of her father into her everyday world. It is vital to talk about such experiences with children and reassure them that such experiences are positive and can't hurt them:

'My husband who served on HMS *Dido*, died when my daughter Julie was two and a half years old. When Julie was eight, we were in the kitchen one morning and she exclaimed, "I saw Daddy standing there last night."

'I had a guest over at the time. We were dashing to school, so I didn't get a chance to ask Julie until the evening. I wanted to have plenty of time with her in case she was worried or wanted to ask any questions. She was adamant about her experience, but accepted it as quite normal. "Oh yes, I saw Daddy. He was wearing white knee socks, a white shirt and shorts. He was smiling at me."

'We had a few photos of my husband when he was serving abroad wearing his overseas uniform, and when I showed my daughter she said, "Oh yes he was wearing those things when I saw him."'

Kath's own earlier experience perhaps helped her to accept Julie's as quite natural:

'I saw my own father five weeks after he died. Dad always doubted there was an after-life, and said it would be very overcrowded in heaven. But he promised to come back and let me know if there was anything beyond. He said that if he didn't appear I would know there was nothing after death.

'My father had been ill for a long time before he died, so the end was a release. I'd had a special Mass said for my dad on the night he visited me. There was a noise above my bed and I woke up. Dad was standing there in his favourite fawn jumper and fawn trousers. At first I was shocked, though not frightened and then I was pleased because I knew he had kept his promise. I was awake. I have had dreams about people who have died, and this was very different.'

Kath's daughter was lucky that, unlike many children, her words found a welcoming response. Many older people I meet can recall, 50 or 60 years later, how they were accused of telling lies, or punished for trying to share the joy of seeing a loved granny or parent.

When a child or young person is mentally disabled, his or her psychic experiences can be taken even less seriously, and regarded as a symptom of their condition. Yet in Chapter 10, Jo describes how her sister, who has Down's Syndrome, has deep spiritual and psychic insights.

I received the following call on a phone-in from Sunderland. Sue told me:

'My mum died, leaving me and my adult Down's syndrome sister, Gail. Gail understood that our mother had died and was not coming back. But whenever we passed the bakery where my mum used to work, Gail would smile and wave. She insisted she could still see Mum behind the counter. She did not see my mother anywhere else.'

As a society we venerate logic and learning almost to the exclusion of the human spirit. The issues of illness and disablement are fraught with difficulty. When we die are we automatically healed, or is it a gradual process? My own daughter Miranda, who saw my disabled aunt at the point of her death, saw her without her wheelchair a few weeks later. Spiritualists do believe that we are healed in the after-life. However, people who have no such knowledge or connections may also spontaneously remark how well a dead relative looks when he or she appears in a post-death dream or vision.

Tom's handicapped son died after a long illness. One day Tom felt his son's presence in the house. "I walked in and Tony was there. I knew it though I did not see him with my physical eyes. "I'm all right now, dad. I'm well and whole again" he was telling me.

So reassuring was the moment that Tom went straight to see his wife at work to give her the good news.

The death of a handicapped relation can be sad since we may see them at the last, suffering. The same sorrow after a relation has died after a long, painful illness is that we remember his or her pain, not the person we once knew and loved.

Everything had gone wrong in Ellen's life. Her daughter was ill and her marriage was in trouble. There were also serious money problems. Ellen was contemplating leaving her husband. One night she woke up and her late mother-in-law Beth appeared at her bedside. During her last illness Beth had turned grey-haired, wore glasses and had been very frail. Now, Ellen said, she was young and fair-haired and looked very well.

Beth smiled and assured Ellen, "Everything will be all right. I promise if you just stick at your marriage through this bad patch, it will be right again. You will get over the money troubles very soon, so don't worry."

Ellen did try hard with her marriage, and sure enough everything improved dramatically and the money worries were resolved. However, what did stay with her was the difference in her mother-in-law's appearance, which she would not have expected.

Kate lives in Scotland, and her mother died when she was 11. However, Kate says her mother often comes to see her just for a chat:

'When my mother first died she would come to me in dreams and talk of everyday things. She looked as she had been in her last illness – care-worn and frail. But as the years have passed she has changed so much, looking healthier every time I see her. I last saw her a few weeks ago and she looked in the prime of her life. The troubled look of everyday problems, the tiredness and frailty are gone. It is wonderful to see her so well and happy.'

Kate has also seen her father twice. The first time he appeared she was at a loss how to react, and like many people was frightened. She says:

'I am just an ordinary housewife with no special powers. About 13 years ago, not long after my father died, I went to bed but could not sleep. I turned over to get comfortable and saw my father's face near the wall. I could just see his head. I felt terrified and thought I must be dreaming, so I closed my eyes tightly and expected him to be gone when I opened them. But he was still there. I turned my back on him for the rest of the night, and by the morning he had gone. I felt he wished to speak to me but could not.

'After about two years I had a dream where my father took me to a place I did not know. In the dream we arrived in a garden. I cannot remember how we travelled. We went down some steps and into a cobbled yard filled with garden tubs containing shrubs and flowers. Railings surrounded the yard. Other people were walking and talking in the garden, yet it seemed totally silent. I asked my father where we were and he said, "I just wanted to show you where I lived. It's all right, isn't it?"'

No one has proof whether we survive death in a form in which we retain our earthly personality. Stories of dead grannies, parents and children returning can be written off as anecdote and trivia. Yet in the absence of hard evidence either way for life after death, the homely tales of family love may offer more reassurance than any scientific theory of dying brain cells and wish-fulfilment. Most families have a story to tell of some family member coming back to offer love or just to say hello, and it is hard to ignore such a mass of human experience. Love for family and partners is a very powerful emotion. Might it not just be strong enough to survive death?

Finally Rachel, a curator at one of Britain's most famous stately homes, offers the hope that we can have fun in the after-life:

'My niece regularly sees her dead grandad. He sits on top of her wardrobe swinging his legs.

'"Do get down, Grandad," she scolds him.

'But Grandad is enjoying his new found freedom.

'"It's nice up here," he replies with a grin.'

# 6

## SENDING A SIGN

M aurice Gibb of the Bee Gees frequently has the feeling that his dead brother Andy is around during recording sessions in the family studios in Miami. Maurice told *Hello* magazine in January 1995:

'One day I was doing the vocals for one of the tracks from the last album, when I heard a creaking noise behind me. I turned around and I could see through the glass booth that the swivel chair he always used to use in the studio had turned round of its own accord. The same thing happened half an hour later so I know Andy's around, which is very comforting.'

Andy Gibb died of a heart attack in 1988, aged 39.

Many people would be frightened or distressed if they saw a dead gran or parent. I believe that we all get the kind of contact we are happy with and that those we have lost would wish for. No loving relation is going to deliberately frighten you by appearing. Nor should we feel that if we do have a vivid dream, smell a mother's favourite scent or hear sounds that evoke our loved one, we are in some way less loved or loving than those who see with their physical eye, a relative who has died.

I recently received a letter from a woman who had been

promised by a clairvoyant that within 12 months she would see and hold again the infant she had lost. Such information is irresponsible, and may actually block spontaneous signs that death is not the end. Others have told me they have found it disturbing to be told that their granny is always there watching them. Our relatives do not suddenly turn into policemen when they die, and we should not let anyone dictate the nature of what is a personal link. Some people do find a good medium helpful in the initial stages of grief, but many do establish a personal way of relating to a person who has died, either with fond memory or something more.

The most subtle contact is a sudden scent, perhaps at times of stress or loneliness, to remind us we are not alone. Jo, in Chapter 10, recalls the strong sense of lavender that heralded her grandfather's presence. Sheila had a similar experience:

'When my father died it was winter and the body was in the house. The wreaths were everywhere and many were of mimosa. From that day I hated the smell of mimosa.

'When my mother died a few years later, I suddenly smelled mimosa though there was none in the house, and I was aware it was my father there to collect her. Ever since I have loved that scent.'

Margaret, who is in her sixties and lives in Bournemouth, told me she could always smell her late father's clean, freshly-washed smell when she was distressed . Her father used to wash himself and his hair whenever he was anxious. The answer to Margaret's dilemma invariably comes in an unexpected way when she has sensed her father's presence.

Occasionally the sign can be less conventional, and yet is such a personal symbol of a certain person that we know that they may be trying to tell us something. Margaret's son was in the middle of a divorce. Suddenly Margaret smelled her late uncle's favourite brand of tobacco. She did not see *him* but an elaborate paintbox, which did not make sense since her uncle was not an artist. But after a moment she made the connection.

Her uncle never went out shopping. It was a family joke. He would go to the pub one night a week for exactly one pint and to a church social on another. But one Christmas he absolutely amazed the family by producing a beautiful paintbox he had bought for Margaret's son. He never repeated the shopping trip. Margaret realised he was saying that he was still watching over his favourite nephew, and things turned out well.

On another occasion, Margaret saw her late mother's two favourite Chinese vases. They used to be kept in her mother's porch but had been stolen. What could it mean? It was summer and Margaret had been leaving her front porch open. She had two similar vases. A subconscious warning or her mother reminding her to be careful and lock up?

The psychic is not always about life and death decisions but can deal with issues, trivial to outsiders, that make up by far the greatest part of our lives. If your mum used to remind you when you'd forgotten things, or told you to take your mackintosh in case it rained even when you were 40, it may be that after death she is still worrying whether you've left the lights on.

Gila, a businesswoman living on the south coast, told me that her mother died very suddenly at noon one day. The family had thought it was a bout of flu. Gila and her father were very distressed that she had died after only a morning of apparently just being unwell:

'A few weeks after my mother died, I persuaded my father to go to his masonic lodge for the first time, and arranged for a lift back for him. It was the first time I had been alone in the house since Mum's death. I put the car away in the garage at about 6 p.m, as I was not going anywhere that weekend. I went into the house through the door from the garage. I was busy in the kitchen when suddenly the door handle on the door leading from the garage into the house started to turn by itself, as if someone was opening the door.

'The handle kept turning. I was alone in the house and there was no access to the garage from outside. I was terrified – I have no time for ghosts and the like – but after about an hour I decided to pluck up my courage and investigate. As I went into the garage I understood. I had left the car lights full on. Had I not gone in, and I would not have done so during the weekend, I would have had a flat battery by Monday.

'"Thank you, Mum," I said, because that is who I believe it was, reminding me as she would have done in life. I have had no further contact with my mother since.'

We can't verify such signs in human terms to the satisfaction of sceptics, but it is a comforting thought that we may survive death as the people we were on earth and still have time for the small concerns of those we love.

One strange but common method of contact is through clocks and watches. I have come across many stories of clocks stopping at the point someone dies. One theory is that when a person dies they give off some kind of kinetic energy that can affect time-pieces belonging to the family, even many miles away. Perhaps the old song, 'My Grandfather's Clock', had some basis in real experience. A reader may know the origins of the song. If so, I'd love to hear.

David Bryan, who lives in Hockley in Birmingham, told me how his dad stage-managed the family time-pieces:

'One evening a nurse phoned my house to tell me my dad, who was in hospital, had suddenly died at 6.10 p.m. My wife and I went round to tell my mother and then we went for a drink at the Railway Pub. During the evening someone asked me the time. I looked at my watch, and it had stopped at 6.10 p.m.

'The police contacted my brother Colin in Sunderland, and when I spoke to him on the phone the next day he told me that his watch had stopped at the time Dad had died. Colin drove down to help me with the arrangements. A couple of days later Colin and I had to go to Dad's house to get his pension book to send back. The first thing to hit us was Dad's old clock. It had stopped at ten past six.'

If a certain object is a family joke then it may well be a way of reassuring those left behind that laughter as well as love survives death. In Anna's family her father's concern with his precious grandfather clock was a standing joke. When he died from a sudden thrombosis, her mother heard him say, "I'm not dead am I?"

"I'm afraid so, old chap."

"What shall I do?"

"Turn round and you'll see someone waiting to meet you."

Her father disappeared. A few years later Anna was in Leeds and her mother in London at home. Suddenly Anna saw her father standing in the doorway laughing. Anna noted

the time and wrote to tell her mother, as the incident mys-
tified her. Her letter crossed with her mother's. At the precise
moment Anna had seen her father laughing, her mother had
heard a crash. The grandfather clock had fallen down. It was
her Dad's pride and joy. Only he was allowed to wind it up, as
otherwise he said they would knock it over.

But it was not Anna and her mother's only shared psychic
moment. Anna says that her mother was always very psychic.
During the First World War, Anna's mother was bathing the
baby by the fire. Suddenly she looked up at the window as if
she recognised someone outside. Anna recalls that she
followed her mother's glance and saw a man outside dressed
in a soldier's uniform. It was Uncle Bulger, a close family
friend. But Uncle Bulger was away fighting on the front. News
came soon afterwards he had been killed in action.

A sign can also help us to put things right after a relative's
death. The signs can be very strange – in the case of Gladys's
mother, nothing less than a Union Jack. Gladys, from the Isle
of Wight, rang me after a radio programme to tell me her
story:

'My mother, who was 92, was into astral projection and the
occult generally. When she was dying, she insisted she did
not want to be buried in the ground. She wanted to be cast out
to sea and her coffin draped in a Union Jack.

'When she was buried we had a conventional funeral, and
as the coffin was lowered into the ground I felt uneasy. Seven
months after her death I was walking my dog along the shore,
thinking about my mother and feeling guilty about her
funeral. Suddenly the dog started scratching the sand and
unearthed a large, intact Union Jack. I found a large stone,
wrapped the flag around it and cast it off a point into the sea. I
felt it was my mother's way of contacting me, and I was able to
give her the sea burial she wanted after all. After that, I felt
totally at peace.'

Dreams, too, can act as a bridge for us to accept comfort
from those we have lost. Psychic dreams tend to differ from
ordinary ones in their quality and intensity. We have all had
vivid dreams that stay with us all day, and yet those who have
had psychic dreams, myself included, say that these are more
like a living experience during sleep. For Colin, one such

dream helped him to come to terms with his father's sudden death. His niece, Rita Laws, lives in Oklahoma in the US. She explained:

'My late grandad appeared to my favourite uncle, one of his sons, in a dream, not long after his death. Uncle Colin is not one to put a lot of stock in dreams, symbols or para-psychology. But after the death of his father he told everyone in the family about the dream that was so real to him he would never forget it.

'Grandee was on top of a high building, and he wanted to come down. But he was weak, sick and couldn't talk very well. Uncle went to him and tried everything to get him down, but Grandee was too heavy for him to take down the stairs or even into the elevator. Uncle even considered taking him down the drainpipe on the outside of the building until he realised it would never support their weight. As he accepted with great sadness that he could not help his father, he woke up.'

Bereavement is a powerful trigger that can reawaken the psychic side in men that many, perhaps, had to leave in childhood. Older men may have less need to rely on logic, and can more easily acknowledge their spiritual nature. I found Stan's story in a very old box of archives at a research centre. Stan is in his seventies, and was devastated when he was left alone after many years of marriage. For him his dreams of his wife were a link between them:

'The dreams of my wife coming to me are of the most extraordinary comfort, and I have the strong feeling she is trying to reassure me all the time. Our marriage was as deep as any marriage could be. Immediately after Sylvia died, and for at least a month after, I dreamed of her nightly, and have been experiencing what I can only call meaningful dreams intermittently ever since.

'The first outstanding dream occurred within a month of Sylvia's death. She was lying on the bed beside me. The bed was flat, with the pillow taken away and the bedspread over it, just as it had been ever since Sylvia had died. She was wearing the nightdress she wore at the end and I knew that she was dead. Sylvia was restless and tossing and turning. I begged her to calm down and lie quietly, whereupon she said, "Do you think I ought to go over now?"

'I replied, "Yes I do, but before you go tell me that you love me."

"With all my heart, I do," my wife said, and as she spoke her face changed to the face she had when she was young. I woke up crying.'

How can we know for sure if a vivid dream is a psychic contact? There are no guarantees, and often the search for verification can detract from the meaning of the experience. The most moving dreams are so personal and reassuring that it is an insult to try to explain them away or probe for proof. And yet occasionally details of which we were not aware can emerge in a dream.

David died after three days in intensive care, after a motorbike accident, when he was still a teenager. One night Don, his father, saw David in a very vivid dream, in which his son was wearing a distinctive tee-shirt with the motif of an eagle that Don had never seen before. Don told his wife about the dream, and she told Don that David had bought the tee-shirt very shortly before his death.

Another sign the family had that their son had survived death was one that, like most of these personal symbols, had meaning only to the family concerned. When David was alive, he infuriated his parents by regularly touching and tilting three pictures on the stairs as he went up. After his death the pictures would still be regularly tilted no matter how many times David's parents straightened them. On one occasion too, they heard the door open and the sound of David whistling as he used to in life, going up the stairs. Don, an atheist, turned to religion as a result of his experiences, which confirmed for him that death was not the end.

As I said earlier, for some people a visit to a medium or a spiritualist church can be immensely comforting. It is important to go to a recognised church or medium and not pick a name from the paper, unless you know of someone who was happy with him or her. Above all, it is vital not to expect too much. If we can be satisfied with a single phrase or symbol then the medium will not feel obliged to offer more. It can be that at the point at which a medium is trying to please problems can occur, and he or she can unconsciously fill in the gaps with guesses. The only problem is when people go to a spiritualist church in the hope of getting a message, and then blindly follow advice apparently from a dead relative.

One accusation against mediums and spiritualist churches made by doubters is that the messages are so general that they could apply to anyone. However, I have come across many cases where the medium has been able to give an idiosyncratic sign that could only apply to a particular seeker, and what is more, gives information the recipient did not know. This rules out the theory that a medium operates purely by reading the subject's mind, which in itself would be very remarkable.

Bernard told me how his mother Bess had gone to a spiritualist church for the first time not long after his grandad died. The medium told Bernard's mother they must not throw away her father's old coat that was hanging behind the hall door as there was money in the lining.

After the meeting, Bess went round to the old man's house to fetch the coat that did hang on the back of the hall door, in itself not unusual. Bess had got rid of all his old clothes, but the coat had been forgotten. There was no money in the pocket and the lining was not ripped. However, Bernard's mum decided to rip the lining open as the coat was too old to hand on. There was quite a sum of money neatly sewn into the lining that Bernard's grandad had obviously been saving for a rainy day.

Barry, who lives in Luton, and works as a prison officer, went to a spiritualist church for the first time at the invitation of a colleague. The guest medium asked him if he knew a woman called Lola. His late grandmother, to whom he had been very close, had that name. The medium went on to describe how Lola used to tap his back pocket and laugh when he was young. Barry knew it must be his grandma.

Every Saturday afternoon when he was young Barry would go to his grandparents' house. His grandmother would take him into the kitchen, wrap a ten shilling note or some coins in a ball of paper, slip it in his back pocket, tap it, laugh and put her fingers to her lips. It was their little secret, as he was her favourite grandchild.

Years later the old lady developed Alzheimer's disease,

and her only knowing contact with the outside world was when she saw Barry. She would tap his back pocket and laugh, recalling the old ritual between them. Barry feels his grandmother is close.

Many older spiritualists have a rich family tradition of helping others to contact dead relatives. Of course, there are those who fill in the gaps with creative guesses. But it is as easy to be too sceptical as too gullible, and if you do visit a spiritualist church you should ask questions but be prepared to listen to the answers.

Take the sure-fire certainty of the very old lady who sits in the centre of the front row every week, inviting the visiting medium to get off to a flying start with, 'You've got a mother in spirit.'

I attended a local spiritualist church for several weeks while researching this book and, true to form, every visiting medium homed in on one particular old lady in the front row at the local church and her obviously departed mother. Was it just, as I suspected, a case of the easy option? Or was mum coming through each week with something to say? Joyce, the daughter, turned out to be a retired platform medium herself.

'It's only recently I've been having messages from my mother via other mediums,' she said. 'I've always been able to talk to my mother directly since her death, but recently I've not been well and have been feeling a bit down-hearted so it has been rather nice to hear from my mother via the platform.

'My mother herself saw my father after his death. It was in a railway carriage travelling from Glasgow, and he told her she must stop crying and grieving because she was holding him back. But Mum was totally inconsolable, and so Dad came to my sister one night and told her to tell Mum that she must let him go on.

"Tell your mother to get off the floor crying and get on with life," he said.

'My sister didn't like to tell Mum. However, Dad was pretty persistent, because a week later a neighbour invited Mum to a small spiritualist circle because she said the group kept getting her husband through asking for her. Mum went very reluctantly and a message for a Maggie – which was Dad's name for her – came through. Mum was sitting on the outside not joining in. Dad told her that he was in a wonderful place, a lovely garden and he told her the friends he had met, old names whom the people in the circle could not possibly have known. "But I'll wait for you," he promised. "I'll not go on without you."

'Some time later Mum went a spiritualist church in a different area and an identical message came through, the same flowers, the same garden, the exact same friends who were with him, and that Dad would wait for her till she came over.

'After that Mum sometimes went along to different churches, and whenever there was a message from Dad for Mum, whoever the medium was and whatever the church, Dad would always be the first message of the evening – don't ask me how he managed to get to the front of the queue.

'Soon after my mother died I had a very vivid dream. They've taken everything from me," she said, even my wedding ring."

'I'd had a new ring made for my anniversary. "You have my ring, mum," I said, and when I woke up it was gone.

'I was very upset as it was so special, and turned the bed and bedroom upside down as my husband was away. But there was no sign of my ring. Then I remembered the dream.

'And the very next day, inside the pillowcase where I'd definitely checked, there it was. I swear Mum borrowed it!

'Mum's first engagement ring (she was engaged twice) was a little old-fashioned 18-carat ring set with three small stones. But though my sister had sent it to me some months before her death, it didn't fit as my knuckles had swelled with arthritis. I kept the ring in a jewellery box as a very precious reminder of Mum. It was Mother's Day, and I'd been regretting that when I was young it wasn't the custom to give mothers presents and now it was too late.

'At church that night, the message came that I had my mother's first engagement ring, but that I kept it in a jewellery box because it didn't fit and that I'd been wishing I'd done something special for Mother's Day, which had been my exact thoughts.

'Another day I'd been thinking strongly about the old-fashioned range we had in the kitchen. I'd insisted we had it taken out in my teens for something more modern, but nothing was so comforting as the old kettle singing on the open hob, and Mum always used to say, "Put the kettle on the range and we'll have a nice cup of tea", whenever things went wrong.

'As the years went by it became a bit of a joke with Mum and myself, to say, "Put the kettle on the range", even when I had a modern stove and I'd come to discover lots of the old things were best after all. The week the message came I had been feeling very low and just wished we could put the kettle on as in the old days and right the world. So when the message came through about the old range and me putting on the kettle now whenever I felt low, I knew Mum was there. It was just what I needed to hear.'

'It's not the importance of the message, and I know lots of people would say, "Oh, my mum said that as well", but if the message comes at the right time and reminds you of an old joke, you know it's meant, and that's the important part. Your family do still care about the ordinary things you're doing and feeling, even if they aren't with you in the flesh.

'I feel very close to my mum. I'm getting more tired now and not so busy with the outside world. I think you can move closer to loved ones in spirit, especially when there are not many of your own age left alive. And when I get a message of love from the platform, it is very uplifting. I've seen so much evidence in my own work that I've got no doubts at all my family will be waiting for me. But of course, that's not to say I'm not afraid of dying, because so many people do go in pain and I don't want the pain.'

It is very easy to forget that spiritualism or any religion is no proof against the fear of dying or pain. And as Joyce pointed out, it's easy to dismiss a message as 'Oh, that could apply to anyone', or 'She's bound to have a mother in spirit at her age'.

Someone may have gone along to the church because they are feeling sad or lonely, and the right words or a special phrase that may sound trivial or even hackneyed to an outsider, may be uplifting. Love can't be quantified and stripped down to a questionnaire or set of statistics.

Finally, it's not all hearts and roses on the other side. A dead relative can be angry on a loved child's behalf. Beatrice was in her mid-forties when her husband Gerard deserted her for a younger woman. In desperation Beatrice went to a medium in London, with the unspoken question 'Will he come back?'

The reply came back loud and clear from her Aunty Agatha, who had lived next door when Beatrice was a little girl and had helped to bring her up. Beatrice regarded Agatha as a second mother, and remembered her anniversaries and birthdays without fail, putting her aunty's favourite red roses on her grave. Now Aunty was flaming mad ' at the man who had broken her little girl's heart, and threatened blood and thunder upon his wretched head.

Regrettably Gerard didn't report back to his ex-wife on the subject. However, Aunty gave Beatrice very sensible advice – to dry her tears and get on with her life, 'Advice, unfortunately, which I didn't take till many years later,' Beatrice told me.

That wasn't the end of the story. Beatrice recently went to a spiritualist church, having made a dash to the cemetery with red roses because it was Aunty's birthday. A message about the roses came through. It wasn't from Aunty but from Uncle Jack, her real uncle, who had died some years before.

'There are three of us together and it's my anniversary,' came the message.'

Beatrice could recall Uncle Jack and thought he would probably be with his two brothers who had been inseparable. But the anniversary? Uncle Jack persisted, but in the end went off with a message about things getting better and a final remark about the roses that weren't for him. It was only when Beatrice got home that she realised it was the anniversary of Uncle Jack's death.

'He obviously wanted to tell me I'd forgotten him,' Beatrice told me. 'I'll put it in my diary for next year. It's what makes the psychic so believable for me. I went to church hoping for a message from Aunty about the roses, but it was Uncle Jack who came through instead wanting *his* flowers.'

So check your diary – unless you want a brickbat rather than a bouquet from the other side.

# 7

# GHOSTS WHO JOIN THE FAMILY

W hen I was writing *Families are Forever*, I discovered the strange phenomena of former inhabitants of a house who would adopt a particular family who moved into the house. They do not form an attachment with every family. In some cases, a house may only became actively haunted when the living and dead inhabitants interact.

Why should ghosts stay in the house where they spent their last years rather than go to their families after death, or move on? The book so far has concentrated on the strength of the family bond, and the last two chapters told stories of grannies, parents and children who do return to their kindred.

Can it be that in the case of a very unhappy family the ghost prefers to remain in the place where he or she was happy? Or perhaps the ghost was entirely alone in life or grew to depend and prefer his or her own company in later years. Sometimes the former occupants offer protection to the new family or one particular member, perhaps a child. On the other hand the ghost may resent the new residents and cause problems. Usually more than one member of the family is aware of the phantom visitor.

Why should Elsie's father come back to haunt his former home when his own daughter lived nearby, had got on well with him while he was alive, and what is more had several psychic experiences so would not have been worried by his presence? Was he in the end more attached to his former home than his family?

Elsie, who lives in the Isle of Wight, told me the following story: 'When my dad died his house was sold to a family with two young boys. One day my Aunty May met the mother who asked if my dad had died in the house. In fact, my dad had died in hospital, but was very happy in his house. One night the little boys had gone to bed and were playing noisily and jumping on the beds. Suddenly an old man appeared in the doorway and shouted at them to be quiet. Then he disappeared.

'Their behaviour improved at once. I knew straight away it was my dad. He was very strict about bedtimes and always insisted we went to sleep without a sound. The description the boys gave their mother of the cross old man confirmed my suspicions. I never found out if they saw him again.'

Although Elsie believes her mother comes to see her, her father does not appear to her.

Another mystery is why Alice's ghost should go to a neighbour rather than her own son, again with whom she had a good relationship. Sarah, whom I met at a talk I gave in the north of England, was visited by Alice's ghost immediately after the old lady's death. Alice was afraid of storms, and if her son was away or at work when one occurred, Sarah would pop down the road to keep her company. Was this why Alice sought out Sarah's help? Was her son too grief-stricken to cope with his mother's presence?

Alice appeared to Sarah in a vivid dream the night after her death. An immediate lightness filled the room.

"I'm not going in that box," she declared. Sarah explained gently to Alice that she was dead and no longer needed her body. Sarah promised Alice she would go somewhere she would be very happy.

Such encounters are difficult to handle as relatives can naturally get very offended if mum or dad comes back to someone else. In *Psychic Power of Children* (Foulsham, 1994), I wrote of one man who crossed the world after his death to visit a niece he hardly knew. His own daughter, who was the same age and had nursed him, was very upset her father had not come to her.

Alice loved flowers and was very green-fingered. She often complained to Sarah that her son George did not share her gift and killed off every plant he went near. Just before the funeral, Sarah was in her local supermarket. She saw a lovely plant and heard the old lady telling her to buy it for George. Sarah gave it to George on the day of the funeral, 'From your mum', which it was.

George was fortunately very pleased with the gift and amazingly the plant lasted for years in spite of George's worst ministrations. Had the old lady known that George could not cope with direct contact, or are some people more receptive to ghosts? However, this does not explain the previous case, as Elsie was psychic.

Sarah's own family were very open to other world encounters. Her daughter Louise saw her late grandfather from when she was very small. Indeed, she would lean out of the cot, smiling and holding out her arms to someone no one else could see, but whom she later identified as Grandad, when she could talk. When her grandma died, Sarah explained and Louise accepted the situation.

Then one day she asked her mother, 'Why did you tell me Granny was dead? She's sitting next to you in the car, and she's not yellow any more.' Sarah's mother had been badly jaundiced when she died.

A ghost may feel trapped in a house and need help from the living occupants to escape and move on, or perhaps even find his or her family. The ghost Gila saw in her holiday cottage needed Gila to contact her daughter. I have obscured the details in this case as the family of the old lady might find the experience distressing. But it is true, and I have recounted the basic facts as Gila told me because the account does show that hauntings are far from straightforward:

'My husband, I and two friends had rented a house on the Northumbrian coast for a month's holiday from a woman I knew slightly through my work. During the first two weeks, I was aware in our bedroom of the sensation of someone brushing my hair, and no matter where I put my hairbrush it would appear on my bed.

'One day towards the end of the holiday – during which I felt I was being watched constantly in the bedroom – I sat by the mirror putting on my make-up. The rest of the party had gone down to the local pub. I again felt my hair being brushed, and the brush which had been on the dressing table had again been moved to the bed.

"Who are you? What do you want?" I asked.

'An old lady appeared. She told me that she had been pushed to her death on the rocks by the evil spirits who had plagued her during the last months of her life. She had brushed her daughter's long, glossy hair when she was a child, and could not resist brushing mine. However, she had not meant to frighten me.

'The old lady told me she was still trapped in the house by the spirits, and could only escape if the house was burned down. She begged me to tell her daughter the house must be destroyed. Then she vanished.

'I was petrified and arrived at the pub white-faced. The landlord asked me what was wrong, and I told him I had seen the ghost of an old lady – I did not identify her because I did not want to embarrass her relatives who were known in the village. He told me that an old lady who was senile had lived in the house we were renting, and had been found dead on the shore. No blame was attached to anyone and she had died entirely of natural causes. It was considered surprising she had walked as far as the beach, since she was fairly immobile towards the end.

'I did not telephone the old lady's daughter as I did not know what to say, but I heard that some weeks later the cottage had mysteriously burned down.'

Most 'adopted' ghosts are not known, even indirectly, to the new residents. This can be alarming, but on the other hand the adopted invisible family member may prove a guardian angel. Caroline, who lives near Birmingham, told me about the family ghost who saved the family's life:

'At one time we lived in an old cottage close to Anne Hathaway's cottage near Stratford on Avon. One morning I was in bed when I heard someone say in a country accent, "Good morning".

'Although my eyes had been closed, I had sensed someone

in the room with me. It's like when the children come in and you just know they are there when you wake, even if they are quiet and trying not to let you know.

'It was an old lady's voice. My husband was downstairs in the bathroom and I thought he was being stupid until I heard the water running.

A cousin of mine came to stay and heard an old lady's voice say, "Good morning, Stuart." We hadn't mentioned the old lady to him.

'In the middle of one night, my husband suddenly leaped out of bed and dashed downstairs. It was cold, as we had no central heating. Soon he came back.

"You were right, " he said.

"What do you mean?" I asked, as I had not said anything.

"You told me a log had fallen out of the fire on to the mat, and you were right. It was lucky I went down at that moment as it was smouldering."

'I had not spoken, I know. It must have been the old lady. The cottage was thatched and there was only a small window in the bedroom. We could not have escaped in a fire. I am sure the old lady saved us.

'Before we moved, we asked our neighbours about the previous occupant, before the property had been divided into two. Years before, a very old lady, Mrs Smith, had lived and died there. Our cottage was reputedly haunted by a friendly old lady, but the neighbours had not liked to tell us.'

However, it may be that a ghost is troubled by external events and may come for reassurance from the living. Were Brenda and Mary's ghosts disturbed by the air raids ? Brenda was in her twenties and lived in a downstairs flat in North Kensington, London, during the war. The house was one of a row of Victorian terraces. She, her mother and sister Jess would sleep on a mattress underneath the table, as there were frequent air raids and they hated going to the shelter.

Several times, Brenda saw a very short, chubby woman only about four feet three inches tall, who must have been about 70, and wore a butcher's blue apron. Her hair was screwed back in a tight bun. Although the room was dimly lit, the woman was quite clear and solid. The second time she appeared Brenda tried to touch her, but she disappeared.

On the last occasion Brenda saw the old lady, she asked if she could help. The ghost did not reply, but she never came again. Brenda was never frightened of the old woman but was curious as to what the ghost wanted, as she never said anything.

Brenda's older sister Mary had the upstairs flat and also had a ghost, this one a woman in her thirties. The first time Mary saw her ghost, she thought Jess was awake and needed something, as the figure was about her sister's age and height and it was quite dark. The woman was opening the wardrobe door.

"Are you all right, Jess?" Mary asked.

The figure did not answer and seemed to go into nowhere. Mary went straight down to the lounge, still thinking it was Jess, but Jess was fast asleep. After that the woman would often appear at the wardrobe door, but Mary only ever saw her back view.

Were the ghosts related? Had they lived in the house before it was divided into flats? It would have been a very exciting story if the ghosts had alerted the family to danger and saved them from a bomb. But most ghosts are not lifesavers, nor did they necessarily die dramatically. If they were perhaps mother and daughter, were they simply getting on with the lives they had always known, in the place they loved? Or had they come to Brenda's family because the bombs were frightening them, and for a time ghost and present-day family shared the terrors of the Blitz?

Amanda, who works at a hotel near Swindon, told me about the little boy ghost who shared her childhood home. She believes he may have been attracted by the presence of a child in the house:

'When I was very young we moved to an old house in Ruabon that used to be a school. Frequently the hall door would bang open when no one was around and there was no wind. Someone used to blow down my ear, and I would see strange white mists in the corner and I knew, I'm not sure how, there was a young boy around. I was never afraid, as it was a friendly presence, just part of life, one of the family really. I grew up with him and accepted him.

'My dad laughed and told me it was imagination. When I was about eight, the ghost appeared to my dad. The ghost was a young boy wearing a long white nightshirt. It frightened the life out of my dad and he never laughed again when I told him the little boy was there. We were at the house 12 years, and the little boy stayed around the whole time.

'Once I was earwigging and heard the neighbours talking about our ghost. The previous owner, an old lady, had never heard or seen him, but he was legendary to the house. I wondered if, as I was a child, the little ghost was attracted by my toys. The only problem was I would be blamed by my mum for leaving marks on the brasses. But I never did. It must have been the ghost.'

Unlike Amanda, Joanne, who was living in Yorkshire, was terrified by her child ghost, who seemed drawn to her son:

'I bought a musical cot toy for my daughter, who sadly was still-born. After her death I packed it away. Four years later my son David was born. I put the toy above the baby's cot. The elastic was high up for safety, too high for him to reach. He was also too young to move or have the strength to pull it. Suddenly I heard its tune, "Frère Jacques", playing very fast, not as it normally does, slowly and gently.

'When I went in, the string was going up and down as if someone was pulling it. I was petrified and ran out into the street. The police were at the end of the road. I called them and said, "There's something in my little boy's room."

'They did not believe me. It happened again, the musical toy playing and the string being pulled up and down by someone I could not see. I threw the musical box away. After that I nailed up the door of the baby's room and he slept with us. Two weeks later we moved as I could not stay.

'I told a neighbour, a woman in her sixties, about the haunting, and she said that years before a little girl had died in the house.

'Three years later we moved to Bristol, and I went to see a clairvoyant. I did not say I was married or had children and I was wearing no rings. She told me about the night when the musical toy played and said it was a little girl ghost who had not meant to frighten me. She had been looking after my baby and had wanted to please him. Certainly he was not hurt at all by the incident.'

Many people find the idea of child ghosts haunting houses distressing. Why are the children not with their grandmothers or mothers, especially if they come from a long-past era? As a mother, I believe that children who die are cared for after death, either by a granny or another loving relative. I am not a spiritualist and yet the more I write the more the idea of a personalised universe seems to make sense to me. I could not bear the idea of children wandering alone and unhappy. I would welcome any thoughts from readers.

Pearl's young ghost, however, is not at all unhappy. He or she just wants a cuddle. Pearl, from Staffordshire, has lived in an 80-year-old terraced house for ten years. Her tiny ghost gets into bed:

'One day I met the lady who had lived in the house before we did. She asked me if I had ever heard a baby crying. I hadn't, but I have regularly felt a toddler crawling up the bed, like a child on his knees, and his little hands feeling the way. When he gets to the top he or she goes away. The child is not only there at night. My husband is a night worker and feels him too. I've even pulled the bottom duvet right up like an apple pie bed, but the child still crawls up to me.

'It's only in the bedroom, but I feel as if someone is watching. It's just like when my own children used to crawl into bed in the middle of the night. I went to the local vicar, not because I was scared but I felt the child should move on, as I hated the idea of him wandering around. He asked what I expected him to do. I said, "If I want bread I go to the baker, and if I want a spirit sorted out, I come to the vicar".

'But he did nothing. A spiritualist told me, "You've got to remember it's their home too," and that made it better. The little ghost is quite friendly and does not seem at all sad. But I wonder why he or she is there, and it upsets me to think of a small child alone.

'This is not my first psychic experience. I used to sense my grandad when I was young, after he died. He used to come to dinner at our house every Sunday. The Sunday after he died we heard his knock at dinner time, "It's only me, girl," and we all looked up because we heard him clear as day.

Then we remembered he was dead.

'I don't feel Grandad now, but I know he would be there if I needed him. My mother and her sister knew when my uncle died. He had been at Dunkirk but survived. Two weeks later they heard his boots running up the passage and said, "That's Alfred", though they knew he could not be at home. Then they felt him dying, and soon afterwards heard he had been killed at that moment in an accident with a lorry on the Great North Road. He was only 19 years old.'

If you do have a friendly ghost who has adopted you there is no cause to worry. A few adopted ghosts can, however, be a nuisance. I've come across many cases of ghosts who insist on tidying things away, to the irritation of the present owners who can't find their possessions, or find that the ghost insists on keeping the tea bags on the top left-hand shelf. Therese, who lives in Londonderry, in Northern Ireland, told me about her 'hoarding ghost':

'My grandfather bought our farm 50 years ago from a family called Harman. It was rumoured the Harmans had put a curse on the land, and after they went people who lived there suffered runs of bad luck. The farmhouse was knocked down about 20 years ago and a bungalow built, next to which was added an office. The office is now the flat in which I live. My parents divorced and I am the only one who stayed.

'Soon after I moved in, ornaments started to be moved and disappear. Overnight £100 disappeared from a file, though the house was locked and no one could have broken in or has a key. I have searched everywhere, and there is no logical explanation as to where the money has gone. One night I was convinced the money was in the loft. I was really angry and determined to get it, but as I went to go up into the darkness I was sure the presence was up there waiting, and I changed my mind.

'The ghost has played a trick like this before. The bungalow beside my house used to be rented to my cousin John, his wife Martina and her sister Eleanor. John and Martina were starting up a riding stables at the time, and all three wore jodhpur boots for work. Every evening the three of them would kick off their boots in front of the fire, and there they would stay until the next morning. One morning, John,

Martina and Eleanor came down to find that one of each pair
of boots had disappeared. This remained a mystery for some
time. Some old jumpers had also vanished.

'One evening while I was visiting, the mystery of the missing boots cropped up in conversation. John suggested we all
concentrated at the same time to see if the boots would reap-
pear. The next morning they all made a dash for the fireplace,
but to their dismay the boots had not come back. Eleanor
went to change the washing over to the dryer. In the dryer
she discovered a plastic bag, and inside were the odd boots
and a couple of the missing old jumpers. The bungalow was,
of course, on the cursed land. However the £100 is still
missing.'

John, from Birmingham, only saw his family phantom once,
but did not like him at all:

'In 1940-41 I was at my mother and father's cottage. It was
summer and a lovely sunny day. I was sitting up in bed getting over measles, and trying to do a jigsaw puzzle.
Downstairs I could hear my mother doing the washing in the
zinc bath. My bedroom door was slightly ajar.

'Suddenly the brass door knob was turned and the door
opened very, very slowly. I thought it was my mother playing
a joke, even though I could hear her pounding the washing
downstairs. A small and wizened old man came into the
room. He was not much higher than the door knob, and wearing a tweedy and very worn jacket with a dark greenish silk
scarf around his neck. He had a very malevolent smile on his
very ruddy and weatherbeaten face.

'As he came towards the bed I yelled out for my mother.
She came running up the stairs, and he just seemed to vanish
into thin air. Of course, she didn't believe me. How could anyone get into the cottage without her seeing them? She had
been working by the only available door. She laughed and
said it was my imagination and went back to her work.'

John's ghostly lodger only appeared once. However, when
an evil presence is more persistent, it can make the present
inhabitants very unhappy and frightened, especially if there
are children in the family. In Chapter 11, I talk about dark
experiences that seem to be fuelled by destructive family
relationships or unresolved anger. Fury against strangers

rarely reaches the heights of family disputes, and most murders are domestic ones. However, if a ghost is unhappy then even if he or she is not malevolent, their presence can be very disturbing.

June was living in a flat in Lichfield, near a strange old church, where the bells would sometimes ring in the middle of the night. Her spectral tenant took more than a friendly interest in her, but June was absolutely terrified:

'About six or seven months after we had moved in, the sideboard began to shake and rattle at midnight. My husband worked nights. The first night I thought it was the traffic, although the road was quiet and I was in a block of flats. It happened again the next night at midnight, and I was really frightened.

'My friend Anne came the next morning and the sideboard started to move. I went into the kitchen and began washing up. I could feel someone pulling the zip of my dress down.

"Stop messing about," I told Anne, and then I realised she was nowhere near me. Anne told whoever it was to leave me alone and to leave, but he didn't and I grew more and more nervous.

'On Christmas Eve, Anne and I went to midnight Mass at the local church. As we came out, she remarked quite crossly, "Would you mind not holding my arm?"

"I'm not touching you," I replied, and as we turned round we both saw a man in a hooded black cape and a tall black hat standing by a grave. He disappeared into nowhere, but we fled for our lives. I found out that the churchyard was haunted by the man we had seen. Legend has it he loved a woman who died suddenly, and that he never got over it and constantly looked for her.

'I felt the man was connected with what had happened in my flat. My husband only once saw the sideboard move, and he said it was just traffic and did not believe me. But I knew the ghost had touched me and then Anne that night in the churchyard, and I could not live in the area any more. Was I like the woman who had died in some way? I was scared to stay in the flat alone. I insisted on staying with a friend on the nights he was away until we could move. We moved right away from Lichfield.'

Often we don't know who or what is haunting us. For June her experiences in the flat made sense when she saw the man in the churchyard. It may be that her flat was built on the dwelling in which the man once loved and lost. Perhaps the woman had died at midnight, the time the sideboard shook. Maybe the man heard the bad news at midnight? Why a ghost should be attracted to a particular person is often guesswork, plus an enquiry about local legends and history. Sometimes if you can at least understand your ghost he or she may go away.

June's ghost was frightening but not necessarily malevolent. However, sometimes a presence can be malevolent towards the family who occupy the house, in spite of a happy atmosphere among the living. It can be destructive for investigators or those asked to help, to suggest that family tensions must be causing the poltergeist activity. Heather, who lives near Oxford, contacted me because a local vicar who had been asked to help with poltergeist activity, placed the blame on the family. Family tensions are one cause of paranormal disturbances but not the only one, and I have been guilty in the past of opting for this explanation without considering other factors.

Heather had also been told by a social worker who was called in, that the family was somehow causing the problem itself, and that the children were disturbed. But that did not help.

The malevolent presence occupied the top of the house, a dark brooding shadow that seemed attracted by Heather's children, especially her older daughter, Maria, who was then five.

When Maria touched a certain toy, mist would come off her arm and her hands would seem green. The toy is now locked away in a cupboard. While the toy was around, Maria started to have *petit mal* fits, but now they have cleared. Heather believes the toy was responsible. Heather's husband has seen the green mist on the landing and is frightened for the family by the terrible, brooding presence, the inexplicable noises and the looming shadows. Heather didn't want psychic investigators, just peace from the ghost that haunted their nights and darkened their days.

Maria talked constantly about a pig on the landing that carried her to her parents' bedroom. He was in the house, Maria said, because he thought there was water. All this was seemingly a natural invisible friend plus maybe some kinetic energy, were it not for the terrifying nature of the presence. Heather persuaded the vicar to carry out a blessing ceremony in the house, and things calmed down for about two weeks. But then, Heather told me, the presence returned, angry because the vicar had tried to take it away from its home.

Downstairs remains fine, but Heather's younger daughter Trina will not even go upstairs to the toilet alone in the daytime. Trina is three and one night sat in bed staring at the curtains, and telling her father about all the funny lights she could see at the window. The family has lived in the house for ten years, but the trouble began when Maria was 18 months old. There is some mystery about how the previous owners died, apparently tragically, not long before Heather's family moved in. Did they hate children? Is their tragedy fuelling the presence?

I don't think I was a lot of help except to acknowledge that Heather's fears were not irrational. I gave her the telephone number of a reliable healing association I felt might be able to put the house at rest. I never heard the outcome, but it was a lesson to me not to automatically seek the family tension explanation for poltergeist disturbance.

I came across another case of a female spirit who was haunting a maisonette, and causing destruction to the young family. An investigating medium reported that this ghost hated children and was infuriated by the new baby. Blessing ceremonies may help, and trying to find out something of the background of the house or even the land that was there before the house, to understand why a ghost is troubled. Strange though it may sound, understanding the problem does sometimes cure it.

Amateur seances are asking for trouble on a psychic or psychological level. If you have got a problem that will not go away, try your local spiritualist church or an understanding local minister. You may need to ask around for the latter, or even telephone the diocesan office. There is always someone experienced and sympathetic in this field attached to each diocese if your local clergy are unhelpful. Don't part with large sums of money to have your ghost exorcised. Your local spiritualist church may accept a donation gladly, but would never charge a fee. Make sure if you ask a healer to help, that he or she is registered with an association like the Federation of Spiritual Healers.

Finally, remember if you make your ghost too comfortable he or she may move with you. Tricia, a widow who lives in Birmingham, had a ghost who insisted on plumping up the cushions and tidying the newspapers in her bungalow. Pictures and ornaments would be straightened during the night. Tricia was not afraid or worried. In fact, she quite liked having the friendly presence around. Enquiries at the local post office revealed that Doreen, a former home help, had lived there for many years. She had loved her home, and had no family apart from a nephew in Australia.

Tricia met a widower at the over-sixties club and they decided to marry. She moved into her new husband's house, three roads away. On their first night together, Tricia left everything as it was. It seemed churlish to spend their honeymoon night spring-cleaning. However, when Tricia left her sleeping husband the next morning to make an early cup of tea, she saw to her surprise that the papers were tidy and the ornaments were in a straight row. Doreen had moved with her. I never heard if the arrangement continued. I met Tricia at a book signing in Birmingham City Centre and did not have time to get her telephone number, as there was quite a queue. If Tricia reads this, I'd love to know if Doreen is still around.

# 8

# A FAMILY AT WAR

Wartime divides families on a physical level, and yet can strengthen the psychic and spiritual connection. Family members who are in danger and far from loved ones naturally think of home, and it may be that the power of family love gives them the ability to return astrally or to send telepathic messages of reassurance.

Rosina lives on the south coast of England, and has always accepted the shared dreams and foreknowledge that have run through her family life. She told me of a special family experience that her grandmother recalled of her own mother. Such events can be an important part of the rich tapestry of family history and should be celebrated and recorded as any other major family landmark, for often they show a continuing family link:

'It was during the First World War. My great-grandma had gone to bed as usual, but was woken by a hammering on the door and her son Tom, calling "Mother, Mother". Her husband awoke but could hear nothing.

"Tom's away in the Navy," he told her. "You must be dreaming." Great-grandma went down to look anyway in case Tom had miraculously returned on leave. There was no one at the door.

'The next day a telegram came to say that Tom's ship had gone down and there were no survivors.'

What purpose do such experiences serve? As a reminder that at the point of death, those we love can reach us telepathically, however far away, and say goodbye? Some take it as proof of survival after death, that we can shed our bodies and return home to reassure those we love. I have come across so many examples that would suggest they are more than coincidence.

Occasionally such point-of-death visions can contain proof that may even satisfy sceptics. In 1944, Nell's brother Anthony was killed in active service.

Before Nell was quite awake, she saw a vision of Anthony on a stretcher, pale but quite happy. He told her he was all right, but he was worried about his friend Adam, who was very lonely. Anthony named a place in Germany where Adam was. Nell asked her father, who knew Adam slightly.

However, her father assured her Adam was definitely not where she had been told in her vision. By chance news came that Adam was a prisoner of war in Germany, having been captured miles away but sent to a camp at the very place Anthony had named. Then Nell knew she really had seen her brother.

At the moment when a dying soldier appears, the person who sees him usually feels overwhelming love as well as sorrow. But can a loved one at home in wartime influence events far away by sending this love and strength? The airman in the glider and the mother whose son was one of the few survivors of the HMS *Hood* disaster are two examples of this apparent power during war that I mentioned earlier in the book. Ellen, who lives in Hampshire, told me:

'During the Second World War my father was on active service in the trenches. Suddenly there was an explosion and my father was blown into a red-hot shell hole. He could feel his eyebrows and hair singeing with the heat and he was convinced he was going to die. At that moment he had a picture of my mother and myself, and he told my mother, "I'm going to die, Jess."

'At home in England, my mother woke up and saw my father in the room. She believed he must be dead because he was there. Miraculously he survived.'

Did the thoughts of his family back home give him the strength to survive against the odds? Elaine did not offer this interpretation, and yet her father did come through what seemed certain death. This inexplicable power as accounts throughout the book have illustrated, does exist in peacetime as well as war. Yet it has scarcely been researched.

When bad news comes, then there may seem no hope. In spite of this, a relative may know through a dream or vision that the loved one is still alive. It can be hard to trust such intangible evidence, and yet often the telepathic link is more accurate than official bulletins. In the following two experiences it was the sister of the lost soldier who received the communication. Pat, from Yorkshire, explained:

'I brought my brother Phil up. He got his exams at night school before he was 18 and then joined up. Phil was an observer with the RAF, going on special bombing raids at the beginning of the war, when we were sending about six bombers at a time. It was a terrible time, as all his bright young friends came to see us and died one after the other.

'Phil went back to camp, and at three o'clock the next morning, just after we had a bomb in the back garden, the phone rang. It was my brother's CO, who said that Phil had been shot down and was reported dead.

'Later I went out with my husband in the car, and I saw almost a mirage in which my brother was in a Dutch house with a man in a wide-brimmed hat, knee breeches and a clock at a quarter to two. Phil was sitting on a bench with his collar open. The room was red tiled, and he was with another boy. I heard him say, "Up with the rocket and down with the stick."

'I rang the aerodrome and the CO assured me there was no way my brother could have been in Holland. He had been sent on a special raid to Essen. My brother was most definitely dead.

'I still refused to have a memorial service for my brother, because I was convinced he was alive in Holland. A couple of weeks later, when I was ironing, I heard Lord Haw-Haw give out Phil's name as captured in Crete. I rang the aerodrome again and the CO agreed it might be him, as the Germans sometimes gave out erroneous information about location. My brother and I had an unusual surname, so the officer looked through the service records and there was not another sergeant with that name.

'A few days later Lord Haw-Haw gave out another unusual name, belonging to another member of that crew. I knew I was right, that my brother was alive.

'Eventually, after a terrible time of suffering for him and waiting without news for me, my brother returned home after the end of the war. He had become a special prisoner, as he had written a thesis at Cambridge on nuclear fission and the Germans thought he knew more than he did. He returned with peritonitis and weighing only five stone.

'What happened was the plane was hit and set on fire. The pilot panicked. The others got out and my brother tied the pilot to a parachute and got him out, and had to come down himself holding on to the harness of the chute, which did not open. They were blown hopelessly off course and landed in Friedburg in Holland. Phil and his friend were picked up at a quarter to two by a Dutch farmer and taken into his red-tiled kitchen. Phil was then handed over to the Gestapo. The farmer wore a large hat. Lord Haw-Haw had lied when he said Phil was in Crete.'

In spite of the horrors Phil suffered, he did return home. The next story did not end so happily, but is still a powerful example of how family love can shine through wartime tragedy. James appeared at his sister Mary's bedside in Melbourne, Australia, to tell her he was still alive but wouldn't be coming home as expected:

'In September 1944 my brother was attached to the RAAF, and after two years' combat service was due to return home within 24 hours. I was studying for my final degree and had been working hard. I remember falling asleep about 3 p.m. and dreaming a vivid intense experience. It was much more than a dream, as if I was myself taking part in the event. I saw a plane flying over water. Suddenly it crashed. The crew baled out and were swimming in the water. My brother was swimming with two men, one under each arm. The dream then became confused and broken and my brother was in my room sitting in the chair, his clothes dripping water on to the floor. I bent over him, asking, "James, is it really you? Are you all right?"

'He lay there, white of face, with the sun shining on his body. Finally he spoke: "Tell Mother I am all right, tell her that I am all right."

'Within seconds I awoke to full immediate consciousness, and walked out to the kitchen where Mother was washing up the tea things after a bridge game with some friends. I told her my dream. It seemed so odd as we knew my brother was on his way home and should have left the war area.

'Within 24 hours we received word that my brother's plane had been shot down. The incident occurred at the exact time of my dream.

'Then began a period of waiting. It appears that the plane had been directed on a particular mission, for which no other crew had volunteered, on its way home.'

Mary's brother, she later discovered, was taken to a Japanese prisoner-of-war camp. In a second dream she saw his death after he and others had given false information to the Japanese. But that is a private family story. I found the experience in an old archive.

Many ordinary people have extraordinary war stories to tell. I have included a few in this book as an example of the ability of families to survive war.

I have come across many war-time links between brothers and sisters, far more than in peace-time. Under normal circumstances rivalry can block telepathy. However, in war, the closeness in age may well make the sibling left at home, in earlier times usually the sister, closely identify with her brother's danger. Fortunately the telepathic channel can also transmit good news, although Jackie's family refused to believe her.

Jackie, who lives in San Diego, USA, recalled: 'When I was a teenager, my younger brother was in service in Japan. He had written to say that he was being processed to leave the service, and so might not be in touch for some time.

'Exactly two months later, my stomach became upset due to a jittery feeling I had. I couldn't eat supper, and wasn't sure why at first. Then it dawned on me that Woodie would be home tonight or tomorrow. I told my parents, and they became a little angry with me and told me to stop such non-sense. The next day was worse. I sat on the sofa while my parents ate, and wasn't even able to read the newspaper.

'There was a knock on the door. I jumped up and cried, "It's Woodie!" I opened the door and there he was. My parents told me to stop that nonsense, but came running into the room when they heard his voice.

'Woodie had arrived in Ohio very late the previous night and decided to stay there overnight and make the rest of the trip on the electric railway the next day. Otherwise he would have had to get us out of bed to come and get him from the station, as there were no taxis that late.'

Good news can be transmitted psychically in many ways. Donald Grovers, a spiritual healer, described how during the war his sister-in-law received a telegram saying that his brother was missing. She was awake night after night. But as she lay sleepless one night, a beautiful light, which she described as a translucent spirit, came to the foot of her bed. Instantly she felt peace, and knew all would be well. For the first time she slept through the night.

The next morning she still felt at peace, and two days later a telegram arrived saying that her husband was alive and safe although a prisoner.

Why was the message received as a sign that all was well when it could equally have been seen as a sign of death? The problem with interpreting psychic experience except on a personal level is that it is often not even what is seen or heard that is crucial. The accompanying emotions that can't be measured or even described in words seem to determine the message. Some people say, "I just knew". This inner message can often be overlooked in attempts to explain or verify a unique family contact. If a person has not experienced a psychic link themselves, it can be hard to understand. Perhaps that is why philosophers, scientists and academics, who try to study the subject as objective observers, cannot fully appreciate the extent and wonder of the human psyche.

Julia's mother had a visitation that confirmed for her that her son had died but that he was at peace. Julia, who lives in Cornwall, described the vision her mother had when her brother was killed in a Japanese prisoner-of-war camp in Borneo:

'Malcolm and my mother were very close. In the middle of the night she woke and felt that someone was outside the room. She leaned up on her elbow and saw walking from the door towards her, a beautiful shining and smiling little girl. The child was carrying a casket. The figure was so clear and real that my mother spoke out loud and asked, "What have you brought for me?" At the same time she turned on the light to have a better look.

'The child vanished. Mother always felt quite sure that Malcolm had somehow been able to send along this shining little girl as a comfort to her, and to assure her that everything was all right. How she wished she had never turned on the light so the visitation might have been longer. Malcolm was very fond of children, as was my mother.'

One of the most fascinating aspects of wartime is that a seemingly trivial incident may save a person's life. The late Frank Rooke, a teacher and artist, told me before his death how, as a young man, his name was inadvertently left off a wartime roster of men who all went to their death. Are such incidents fate, chance or a personal guardian spirit? Edmund is convinced that his late Uncle Alf was able to protect him from almost certain death, although Edmund had a far from easy war. Edmund wrote:

'When I was 12 I was staying with an aunt and uncle in Lanarkshire. I was playing with my younger brother and cousins in a darkened corridor of the house and I saw quite clearly the figure of Uncle Alf, a brother of my father's who had died there five years earlier. I had known him well so there was no mistaking him. But I upset the household with my claim and Mother was sent for and I was taken home, which was a relief to me as I was somewhat nervous about my experience. However, once home my fears vanished and I had no after-effects. But in later years Uncle Alf was to prove very important to me indeed.

'As an under-age soldier during the First World War I was training at Kinross. Off duty we would lie down on our bunks for an afternoon nap or to read or play cards. This particular afternoon I was resting, in a kind of sleepy state, but aware of my surroundings and the persistent thought came that some-one was trying to speak to me. It was Uncle Alf, and he made it clear that I would be protected from death or serious injury, but that I would suffer and that I would have a leg problem.

'From that time forward I seemed to receive all the good fortune, as if a road was made for me from one training camp to another.

'Instead of going to India, as arranged for the company of young machine gunners, we were hurriedly dispatched to France. I arrived in France in March 1918. I nearly missed the draft with my companions, but eventually was included at the last minute to take the place of a sick youth. We were all only 18. At our base in France the draft left without me. It was a mistake that I was not on the draft.

'Days after, I had to report myself still there, and eventually was sent up with a draft who were all strangers. That unit was to relieve a Company of machine gunners in the line. The front line was broken in the final German drive and we wandered back in retreat. There were dangers but I seemed to have a charmed life, day in, day out. We marched at night, and it was then my leg troubled me. At first it was my foot, and unable to put on a boot, I got hold of an old French slipper.

'Unable to march, I was put on duty looking after the faithful mules. But my foot did not improve and became poisoned, and I had to get medical attention. It was then I had my first attack of French fever. That brought me down the line to base. But in hospital I was very ill and was making little progress. Eventually, I was evacuated with the wounded to England. This was the end of my soldiering days. Unlike most of my companions, I came home alive and suffered no permanent injury. It seems I was protected, as Uncle Alf had told me back in my training camp in Kinross.'

Civilians in wartime can also have a difficult time. Because there is so much danger and stress attached to war, even back home, it can be hard to distinguish a general anxiety from the urgent call within. Yet I have been told several accounts of wartime London where civilian lives were saved when a voice, apparently from nowhere, suddenly warned of imminent danger. Seconds later a building would collapse in the path, or a bomb explode.

Alan was in the ARP and frequently had to go on to bomb sites. One night during the Blitz on Coventry, he heard a voice warn him not to let his family go to the Anderson shelter. Fighting against his training, he told his wife to stay in the cellar of the house. That night, a building close to the shelter received a direct hit and all within were crushed. It was hard for Alan to trust a voice he afterwards believed was his own late father, who had been killed in the trenches during the First World War.

In contrast, Thelma from the Isle of Wight, blames herself many years later for not listening to a vivid premonition:

It is hard having tea in Thelma's neat bungalow to imagine her in war-time China. Only the exotic treasures are a reminder that an apparently conventional retired matron can have a whole psychic world waiting in the wings:

'It was at the beginning of the Second World War,' she told me, 'and we were to move to Canton from Hong Kong so we might be safe from the invaders. My sister and my son were to travel on the ferry from Hong Kong to Canton with the baggage, while I was to follow later with the baby, on an American gunboat.

'The night before they travelled I had the most dreadful dream, that was so real it seemed I was there. I saw the ferry. It was one we'd travelled on before. There was great panic because the ship was sinking and the people locked on the lower decks were up to their chins in water. I saw quite clearly my sister and my son being handed over the side on to the *Tarantula*, a British gunboat that took them back to Hong Kong. Then they were transferred to a smaller river boat to bring them back to the harbour. I was terrified, but I didn't speak out because everyone was nervous of travelling at the beginning of the war. I knew I wouldn't be taken seriously.

'At 8 a.m. my sister and son went to the ship, and I again thought that the dream had been so vivid I should have warned them. At 6 o'clock that evening I was with my parents listening to the radio when a news flash was broadcast. The ferry my family had boarded had been wrecked. There had been 1,200 people on board. It was not known if there were any survivors. I felt like a murderer, that I had perhaps let my own son and my sister go to their deaths and not spoken out.

'There were floating mines, and I knew if the boat had hit one there would be no hope. At 11 p.m. a senior police officer we knew rang to say that passengers were being taken off by a British gunboat, the *Tarantula*, and transferred to a river boat to bring them to shore. My son was only six at the time.

'When I met my sister I said, "Let me tell you what happened," and my dream was true in every detail, It was the English captain who had saved the ship from completely sinking, by running it on to an island in the channel.

'But I never forgave myself for not speaking out in advance and sparing them the ordeal, I was ill for weeks afterwards.'

Dorothy also had a bad war, although she saw little action since she lived out in the country in Wiltshire. At the outbreak of war, her husband had joined the Navy and was drowned some months later. Then her child died, and she returned home, dividing her time between working in the factory and looking after her invalid mother.

After her mother's death Dorothy kept house for her father, who survived his wife by a year. She then had to leave the family house, and moved into a small cottage. By this time she had met and married Simon, who was sent home from the Army as an invalid. Happiness still eluded Dorothy. Simon's condition deteriorated rapidly, and he was admitted to a local mental hospital with a very poor prognosis.

Around this time Dorothy became totally deaf, though doctors could find no reason and therefore could offer no relief. She lived in her damp, dark cottage and sank further into depression. Dorothy was unable to sleep, and at night she would wander around the countryside. She was particularly attached to the stretch of canal close to her cottage, which was a pleasant walk during the daytime.

Dorothy regularly found herself standing at the edge of the canal reservoir formed out of a disused quarry. It was a beautiful place, especially on moonlit nights. One night Dorothy stood close to the edge, gazing at the still, dark water and wondering if she had any future. A voice said loudly and clearly, "Go home, Dorothy and go to bed."

It was her father's voice, and it was the first voice Dorothy had heard for weeks. She had been very attached to her father. Shocked, she stepped back from the canal edge.

Next morning she woke to the sound of traffic and children playing. Her hearing was restored. It was a new lease of life. She found a better cottage and a part-time job. She organised her husband's return home, and once home he improved enormously. Dorothy dated her return to life from the time she heard the much-loved voice of her late father.

Wartime sweethearts offer the most poignant of love stories. So many were parted by death or loyalty to country. Though Otto and Janet were not married, I include their story because families are more than legal ties, as this book constantly shows. Otto, an East German, was interned on the south coast during the Second World War. Janet shared her ongoing love story, that has spanned almost 50 years:

'In December 1947 I was invited to dinner with a senior colleague from work, who had a former German prisoner of war visiting him. It was then I met Otto for the first time. We shook hands and an absolutely wonderful feeling passed between us. Few words were spoken as Otto's English was limited and I knew no German.

'We began our friendship that night and continued to meet. Otto was working as a cook at the camp, He told me he was from a town near Leipzig. For four months we spent our free time walking, dancing and just being together. Rain or shine, he would walk several miles to meet me. Once he arrived soaked and I gave him my old bicycle. He had to get permission from the commandant to keep it.

'The day came when we had to say goodbye, not knowing if we would ever see each other again. Otto told me that life in East Germany was too hard for him to take me there as his wife. He went first to Southampton, but his passage was delayed by 24 hours, and so he managed to hitch back to see me. We spent just ten minutes together before he had to begin the long trek back, and it was the last time we were to be together.

'I had just one letter from Otto after he returned to East Germany – a very sad letter. He had no money or clothes and he had been put in the East German police. My letters and magazines were returned to me after that. By now it was the end of April 1948.

'Two years later I married and had a family, and it was only at odd times and Otto's birthday I would think back to the old days and what might have been.

'It was not till 1970 I got interested in spiritualism, and had moved to a different part of the country. I made a new friend, who knew a trance medium in Leicester. The medium was one of the old-timers and a lovely soul, and we went for lunch with her. Though I had never met her before, she started to say that Otto was there and was sending me love and red roses.

'I was so surprised I didn't know whether to laugh or cry, but at least I knew where he was and had at last made contact again, even though it was apparently after his death.

'Over the next eight years I received messages from different mediums at different churches round the country saying Otto was there, and sending me love and red roses. Everywhere I went a message was waiting, often including small details of our time together – how once he had arrived in the pouring rain and I had given him my rusty old bike.

'Then one day in June 1981 I met a blind healer, who had come on holiday to my area and was staying with a friend. I asked him to hold Otto's photo. He said, "This man is not in spirit. He's still on the earth plane."

'I was lost for words. But I was determined to find out the truth. I decided to write to the East German police in Leipzig. Otto had told me in 1948 that that was where he was based. I suppose I was expecting a lot in view of the political situation.

'A few months later, in February 1982, a letter came. It had been written by a friend of Otto's. He sent me Otto's address. The letter had been posted to me from West Germany and had been folded many times. I wrote and thanked the person, but heard no more.

'I then wrote to Otto, and also plucked up courage to telephone. While we were talking I could hear constant clicks on the phone line. I was sure we were being monitored. It was a difficult conversation.

'I said, "It's Janet from Bournemouth."

'He promised, "I'll write." He did. They were not very forthcoming letters, just a few lines saying he was all right and that his friend Fritz, the other POW I knew with him, had died. Otto told me he, too, had married. Thereafter I received

Christmas cards from Otto and his wife, very polite and formal. We still exchange cards.'

Messages persisted from Otto in the spirit world even after
Janet discovered he was still living. As recently as six months
ago, she received such a message. The medium gave Janet's
maiden name and asked her if she could speak German. He
went on to describe Otto, told Janet that she and Otto were
twin souls, and that Otto was waiting for her on the other side.
This time after the meeting, Janet questioned the medium
and told her she knew that Otto was still alive. The medium
was still convinced Otto had come through from spirit, and it
was not till Janet received the latest Christmas card that she
knew for certain Otto was still alive.

Did part of Otto die when he left Janet behind, and is that
part of him in spirit? Or when he is sitting in his chair in the
evening does he sometimes think of the 18-year-old he
loved? Janet says at times she finds herself saying his name
for apparently no reason. Or is Otto communicating through
his dead friend Fritz? The messages are definitely coming
from Otto, for it is Otto's name that is given. If Otto were to go
to a meeting would he hear from Janet in spirit ? Otto is much
older than Janet. What will happen when he does die? Sup-
posing Otto's wife dies first? Janet is a widow. Will Otto come
to find his lost love, and if so will Janet get angry messages
from beyond?

Janet would like to travel to East Germany to meet Otto one
day, but it is unlikely their love could be rekindled on earth.
Perhaps that is what Otto is saying, that it is only their love
that is for ever, and that only beyond can they be reunited. I
hope to continue the story in a subsequent book.

Finally, in all wars there are natural survivors who seem to
use a keenly-developed instinct to keep one step ahead of
danger. Dorothy, who lives in Bracknell, told me how her
mother used psychic means to keep the family one step
ahead of the Germans:

'My mother insisted on moving house four or five times
during the war. There seemed no reason, but suddenly she
would up sticks and go at a moment's notice. The strange
thing was each of the houses we left was bombed shortly
afterwards.'

# 9

# IS THE FAMILY BOND GENETIC?

J ennifer Moss's daughter rang her mother back after Jennifer had known Naomi was pregnant, in spite of their estrangement. "You can't get away from blood," Naomi said.

Evidence from research carried out in America would suggest that the genetic magnet is powerful. The links between a birth mother and sometimes birth father and a child, separated at birth from his or her natural family, survives even prolonged absence. The lives of the separated parties may follow uncannily similar paths. I wrote about this kinship instinct in my book on the maternal bond, *A Mother's Instincts*.

Perhaps the most amazing phenomenon is how separated parties are drawn together by a link that defies logic or science. The cases in this chapter come mainly from the US, as most of the work on psychic birth links has been carried out there. However, I am starting to receive cases from the UK, and I would be grateful if any readers who have experienced this would write to me.

Al is a paramedic I met in Los Angeles. He did not know he was adopted until he was in his mid-thirties. What he did not know was that the father who brought him up was not his birth father:

'As a kid, from about the age of six or seven, I had a recurring dream for years and years about a man giving me an old book to read. I was sitting at a table or a desk and looking at the book.

'It was nice and large with detailed carvings and pictures, but whenever I tried to read it or see the title, it went fuzzy. The dream went on until I was about 18, when I left home. When I was 33 and happily married with four children, my wife was away and the children were playing in the garden. It was about 6 p.m. There was a knock at the door and I could see a man standing there. I knew he was important to me, though I did not know how. I told him to come in, but he still stood there. My wife was surprised when I told her that I had invited a stranger in, since apparently I did not know who he was. When I focused on the man he disappeared. However, when I didn't, I could still see him. It was the same sensation as the book, where it went fuzzy when I tried to identify it.

'I was very upset over the next couple of weeks, and started dreaming of a voice telling me to look at the old photos and see what was missing. I was also dreamed about an old lady sitting in bed, going through her things. Behind her on the wall were shiny metal objects, pots and pans maybe. When I met my birth gran I discovered she had been dreaming of me during those two weeks, and was under the impression she had found me. Indeed, she asked my birth father if he had heard from my sister and myself (we were twins). When I later went to Florida to see my gran, I discovered that on her wall she had silver photos of all the children, grandchildren, cousins, nieces and nephews, the shining wall in my dream.

'I asked my sister to come over with the photo albums, and we realised that about two years of photos were missing in my mom's life, including our early childhood. My parents admitted that my present dad had adopted us when we were one. I used the Internet, the world-wide computer network, to try to find my birth father. The very next morning I found a single name on the screen, which I knew was him. It was an emotional phone call after 33 years. I did not want to scare him. My father, who brought me up, has taken it very badly, but I needed to be complete.

My birth dad has a sister who lives only 45 minutes away, whom I'd never met. In the photo album was a picture of a house I could not recall visiting. When I visited my aunt it was her house, and I was able to tell her the entire lay-out of her home without seeing it. She used to babysit and I had not been there since babyhood. She was thrilled I had remembered it deep down. If only my mom had told me. I feel so sorry for the people who will never have my chance, and are looking for families they will never find. I am now searching for the book of my childhood dreams.'

Dr. Douglas Henderson, Professor of Psychology at the University of Wisconsin, Stevens Point, and Dr. Lavonne Stiffler, are both involved in research in the US on the links between birth mothers and the birth children they may not have seen for many years. Both experts have personal experience of the subject, and Dr. Stiffler's thesis has been made into a book called *Synchronicity and Reunion* (FEA Publishing, Florida, 1992).

The following two cases were studied by Dr. Stiffler. One adopted woman told her:

'When I was a little girl, and all through my teenage years, I always wanted to be called Maggie. Not for any particular reason. I just always wanted that name. When I located my original name in the state's birth register, I found that it was Margaret. So I really was a Maggie all along.'

Occasionally the name bond can work in reverse, as one mother recalled. 'I had sent for and received records from the hospital where I had given birth to my son 25 years before. Also enclosed were a copy of his footprints. The footprints were what really got to me emotionally. I wrote a poem about him that day, and superimposed copies of his little footprints on the poem. I tacked it to the wall just inside my bedroom door. A few months later, I glanced at the tiny footprints again and the name "Bryan" appeared in my thoughts, out of nowhere. I decided it had to be the name given to him by his adoptive parents, and when we were reunited I discovered his name *was* Bryan.'

I met Professor Henderson while we were both appearing on a US NBC television programme about the maternal bond. We continued to talk after the programme, and he told me of his research into birth mothers and the children from whom they are separated, and of the similarities in their lives:

Don, who lives in New York, discovered his birth mother in Pennsylvania 44 years later. Separated from her since shortly after he was born, he found almost eerie parallels between his life and hers. As Don approached his birth mother's home for the first time he saw two ornaments hanging in the front window, a hand-carved hummingbird and a crystal sun-catcher. The man was stunned because in his own front window he also had two hanging ornaments – a hand-carved hummingbird and a crystal sun-catcher.

Twin brothers, studied by Professor Henderson, who had been separated from birth and raised by different families, again discovered remarkable similarities in their lives. Both men had married women with the same first name, and had given their sons the same name. Each man had become a volunteer fireman and had a dog called Toy.

Professor Henderson commented: 'I believe that such mysterious coincidences cannot be explained by the cause and effect reasoning that is prevalent in western culture. There is no way that genetic similarities could produce such striking similarities. There has to be something going on we don't understand. The explanation for this type of phenomena may lie in another dimension we know little about. To find answers the scientific community will have to explore different ways of studying reality, and its different dimensions. At present, science could be missing out on significant discoveries because it does not have the right methodology for reviewing such a wide range of data.

'In some ways the study of synchronicity (which Jung defined as "meaningful coincidences") can be compared with the study of radio waves at the beginning of the century. Before radios were invented hardly anybody imagined that voices and music could be sent thousands of miles through the air.'

The next morning I met with Dr. MarLou Russell, an eminent Los Angeles clinical psychologist and family counsellor. She told me how she herself had had therapy to work on her early separation conflicts. MarLou found herself recalling, before her birth, arguing with her birth mother. "You can't give me away. I won't let you."

At last MarLou said she turned stubborn and refused to come out. When she met her birth mother years later, she told MarLou she had been very overdue when she was born. I told Doug Henderson and MarLou my own strange story, which until that moment I had never seen as anything other than a childhood fantasy. I am still uncertain.

My father died while I was pregnant with my first child. He was a very sad man, a working class intellectual who was cruelly treated as a child. His mother, a dresser to Marie Lloyd, the music hall star, when she came to Birmingham, was a widow and struggled with various jobs to keep her family. My father was tied to the railings by his childminder and fed on cabbage leaves. As a result he resented his own children, and could behave quite brutally. It was only when he suffered hardening of the arteries of the brain and began having delusions, that I was able to feel any sympathy for him. In the months before his death I came to forgive him. He was so pitiful a figure I could not do otherwise, and so when he died I had no bad dreams.

But that's not to say he didn't come back in a helpful way. A couple of years ago, I had a strange dream in which I was holidaying in a place in Canada, with a huge mass of water. My father was swinging upside down on a crane outside the hotel window. He looked like the young man I had seen in old photos of his youth. His face was smeared with clay. He kept saying, "You do not exist", almost as a challenge.

The dream coincided with a period when I was feeling overwhelmed by my family, and the struggle of writing and running a home virtually as a single parent were proving too much. I had decided I was going to give up writing. In the dream, my father goaded me as he had done many times in life, and out of sheer stubbornness I decided I would carry on.

I had never felt I was connected with my father. My mother hinted that he was not my real father, and she told me a story that came straight out of a romantic novel. Before the war she had been in love with a Canadian called Jack, whose father had a business in Ontario. When war broke out, Jack was called home suddenly. He left a letter for my mother, begging her to join him, and leaving a contact address. Her own mother destroyed the letter before Mum could read it, and it was not until years later that my mother discovered that Jack had not deserted her.

Meanwhile my grandmother had engineered a match with the boy over the road, who moved in, ensuring that my grandmother would be looked after in her own home for the rest of her life. Ironically she died shortly afterwards.

It was said that my father could not have children, and for five years the marriage was childless. In 1947, Jack returned and took my mother for tea in Lewis's, the local department store. Nine months later, I was born and my paternal grandmother and aunts kicked up a hullaballoo, saying that I was not my father's child. Certainly my only brother was adopted. After my mother's death I quizzed her only sister, who lived with us. She could recall a man coming to the door not long after I was born, asking to see me. My mother became very distressed and would not let him in.

Like all the best stories, I always felt I belonged elsewhere, and hoped that my real father would claim me. My dreams were shattered when I went to Canada in 1977. I visited Ottawa, Toronto, Montreal, Quebec and Niagara, and felt no sense of coming home. I did not even know I had conceived my first child, weeks before the holiday; in those days my psychic hatches were well battened down.

On January 17 1994, I was making an *Unsolved Mysteries* programme with NBC, when my world was torn apart by the earthquake. My hotel in North Hollywood was less than ten miles from the epicentre. As well as losing my certainties that the world was largely controllable and predictable, I ended up being flown out of the US almost immediately. I was offered a flight via Seattle. I cannot claim any psychic instincts – I thought Seattle was on the east coast, somewhere south of New York. To my surprise the plane headed northwards. As we flew over the twin peaks covered with snow and Seattle harbour, dotted with islands and small craft, I felt for the first time in my life I was home. Months later I realised Seattle was the place I had seen in my dream.

At the airport, although I knew there was only an hour between flights, I automatically headed towards the exit, with only my small flight bag. I knew exactly where I was going, to a bench by the waterside. I knew there I would find the answer, and that there I belonged.

My sensible,logical side reasserted itself. I had a husband and five children back home, as well as mortgages, overdrafts and three cats, who hated the cheap cat food my husband bought for them in my absence. I came back to England, but feel I have left part of myself there.

Doug Henderson has suggested I try to find my real father through the Internet, but I am hesitating. Perhaps I should take a trip to Seattle and wait on my bench.

Although this psychic birth link is mainly recognised in America, I did meet a woman living only about 25 miles away from my home, who herself had instinctively identified her real mother. Rosemary is in her fifties and lives in Hampshire. She told me she was brought up by two unmarried sisters:

'A lady, Aunty Isabel I used to call her, came to the house once a month when I was very small. I used to miss her desperately when she was not there and cry for her, though we had other visitors who came regularly. I knew there was a special link between us that I could not explain or even understand. It was an instinctive call, though I do not think she felt it or certainly did not show me any special affection.

'The doll she gave me was my most precious possession, although I had plenty of other toys. Then in 1944 Aunty Isabel just stopped coming. I found out years later she had got married. The last time she came, I was three and a half. Although I did not know consciously I would not see her again, I ran into her arms and clung to her, crying.

'I asked every week where she was, and was told she was too busy to come. It left a total hole in my life and I grieved for her. Until I was 13, I pleaded every week for Aunty Isabel to come or that I could go and see her. But my requests were simply disregarded. I never felt I knew who I was. There were so many gaps in my life, so many unanswered questions.

'One day I found a picture of Aunty Isabel in a chest of drawers, and I used to peep at it. One day a nephew of the family who adopted me, caught me with the picture and said,

"Did you know that's your mother?"

'Isabel had given birth to me in 1941, and the man I suspect was my father abandoned her and went to America. Her parents were not told, and a complex web of lies was woven. I finally met my real mother in 1982 at a hotel in Surrey. She did not want to see me. The meeting was very formal and my mother was anxious that her husband and new family would not find out about me. We had tea and scones, and she gradually relaxed and began to talk about my past. For the first time in my life, I knew who I was and I could fill in some of the gaps. I had always felt instinctively drawn to Scotland, and felt I had Scottish connections. It turned out my great-grandad came from Forfar.

'When I saw my mother I felt we were one. I had become a nurse because I had heard Aunty Isabel had been one. I did not enjoy nursing and had really wanted to be a teacher. My mother had wanted to become a teacher and had not enjoyed nursing either. My mother's sister had been a teacher.

'I still feel resentful, as I want to be a part of my mother's life. She spoke my thoughts, but she is afraid and has asked me not to contact her at her home, though I have driven past'.

Even when a reconciliation goes wrong, old memories from early childhood can be confirmed by discovering natural roots. April went back to her native Canadian Indian village when she was 16, after a disastrous adoption by a wealthy Los Angeles family. Her welcome was less than rapturous, and she hated the frozen wastes. At least, as she told me, she discovered that a lot of her early dreams and half-visions of the northern lights shooting through the sky, of riding in a canoe, hunting and erecting teepees in the wild had really been part of her childhood and were not mere fantasies. She regained her lost childhood.

The links of blood are very strong, but the psychic bond is not purely genetic, any more than love is. Adoptive parents also have strong intuitive links with the children they adopt, and these can confirm the rightness of the relationship. Such bonds are not denying the blood link, and it is perhaps a mistake to see the situation as either/or. The love connection is more than genetic, and families are rooted in care and familiarity as well as kinship.

Mothers frequently have pre-birth dreams of their unborn child, and often the details of the child are discovered after birth to have been totally accurate. Adoptive mothers, too, have pre-birth dreams of their children, although they are growing inside another woman. I will recount two such dreams as, I find them perhaps the strongest evidence for an adoptive psychic link. Althea, who lives in New York, told me that she had a dream of her adopted child before that child was even born:

'Before the dream I had wanted to adopt a child from an orphanage in my native Pakistan. But I was very worried about going through the interviews and complicated pro-cedure in New York before I could get the necessary papers to bring a child into the country.

'Usually I do not remember my dreams, but this was very clear and in brilliant colour. In the dream I saw the face of my future child. The face was distinctive in every detail and she was looking at me, for I knew it was a girl and that she would be mine. I woke my husband and told him he must not worry about the adoption and that I would go and see the judge by myself. The judge was wonderful and told  me my future child would be very lucky. I told him I was the lucky one to be chosen by my future child.

'Now I could go any time and choose the baby. I was given an opportunity to travel on January 20. I knew it was not the right time, as my baby had not yet been born. My husband was impatient for me to go to Pakistan but I told him I would know. In the middle of April I started to make plans. My birthday is April 26, and I knew my baby would be born then.

'When I was on the plane, I experienced dreadful labour pains. I had three children already, so I know what the pains are like. I had good labours and enjoyed them, and I knew my baby's birth mother was in labour. Then the pains stopped. I was certain she would not give birth until I arrived. When I reached Pakistan and went to the orphanage, I was offered a beautiful baby boy. I refused because I knew my daughter was there, waiting for me, and I would recognise her instan-tly. My husband back home was disappointed. I had turned a baby down, and he wanted me to take any healthy child, but I knew that my own baby was there waiting.

'A giant of an orderly came down with a baby wrapped so you could only see the face. In his arms was my baby, the child in my dreams. I smelled her and saw her face and hands and feet. The rest was wrapped in a towel.

'The orphanage tries to match the babies, and she was a perfect likeness to me. She was weak but I said I did not mind. She was like a porcelain doll, so perfect. I had to get permission from my brother in-law. He was overwhelmed by her beauty.

'The baby's mother had died at birth. The baby was premature. Her mother had gone into labour at the time I was on the plane. As I had known her labour had stopped, and she had not given birth until I had reached Pakistan. The baby looked at me as she had in my dream.

'My new daughter was born on my birthday, almost to the minute, and she has my husband's unusual blood group. No one believes she is adopted, as she is the image of me. It all started with a dream that led me to my child, and now at 20 months she is so beautiful and intelligent you would never guess she had been a sickly baby. I believe my prayers were answered.'

When I last wrote about adoptive bonds, I mentioned the story of a mother who dreamed of a dark-skinned, dark-haired boy being born to a fair-skinned, blonde-haired woman. When she was given her adoptive child he was the boy in her dream, and had been born at the moment she had the dream, which had been so vivid she had noted down the time. I met Linda and Dick, who come from Oklahoma, and the details were so fascinating that I include them now. Linda had a vivid dream that was more than a dream, almost an out of body experience, in which she was in a labour ward:

'It was so real I could almost touch the woman, a blonde, fair-skinned woman. I watched the baby being delivered, a dark- skinned, dark-haired boy. The moment was incredibly moving, and I was convinced I was witnessing an actual birth. Then I was in my bedroom, wide awake. I noted down the date and the time, although I thought I had somehow witnessed the birth of the child of a neighbour who was pregnant at the time. However, my neighbour had not given birth.

'I told Dick my husband about the dream, and we discussed what it might mean. When we were given Ivan, our adoptive child, he was indeed the child whose face I had seen so clearly that night. The date and time of his birth exactly coincided with my dream. I knew that I had witnessed his birth for a reason, to confirm the rightness of the adoption.

'Sadly, the child's mother died and I was sent some photographs of Ivan from her family. She was the fair-skinned, blonde-haired woman in my dream, and I felt very close and loving towards her as we had shared such a precious moment.'

Dick said that for him his wife's dream drove away any doubts he might have harboured about the adoption, and he knew that Ivan was meant to be theirs. The bonding Dick felt was helpful in all the daily hassles of bringing up any child, which can be even more difficult in an adoptive situation. Most wonderful, the closeness of the bond is not exclusive, for Linda and Dick have encouraged Ivan to see his birth father, and I was shown photographs of them together.

Adoptive mothers, like birth mothers, have telepathic links with their adopted children. Sheila, from California, adopted two girls, Hilde and Davida:

'Davida went on a ski trip from school. At about noon that day I felt a sudden thud on my forehead. I knew something had happened, but could do nothing. I could hardly wait for Davida to come home. When she finally arrived she had a huge lump on her forehead. After hugging and kissing her I just asked, "What time?" She told me that her foot had slipped out of the ski, which had come up and hit her on the forehead – at noon.

'Hilde must have been about 11 years old and I was working part-time. While at work, I was aware that all was not right. I was hyperventilating and worried. I left my desk and tried to relax. I got a somewhat distorted vision of Hilde. I called the school, and Hilde was suffering an asthma attack.

'When Davida was 18, she went to Ireland. She rented a room and worked in a pub for several months. One day I had an overwhelming feeling I needed to contact her. I tried several times without success. When we finally connected she wasn't feeling well, and was in need of some sympathy and mothering. She had tried to reach me but could not get through. We chatted for a while and she felt much better.

Sheila's stories are but a few of several she sent me, all normal intuitive links between mother and child, and remarkable only because the bond is not a genetic one. These links are very precious to adoptive parents in confirming the relationship is right.

Separated children, like Rosemary, whose story is told earlier in this chapter, may feel they are instinctively drawn to their birth mothers. Conversely, a child may be drawn to a member of the family other than his or her natural parents, especially if that relation has brought the child up. In such a case, the parental bond seems to transfer to the relation, who is more distant in blood, but has provided the day-to-day caring of a parent.

Bhajan Singh was linked into his uncle's death thousands of miles across the world, in a way often only the closest of relatives do. He explained:

'I lived with my uncle whom I called father, as he had brought me up since the age of four or five. We lived as father and son. When I came to America to work, my wife and children continued living with him as well as my mom (aunt). I went to visit them all in 1989. When I was leaving, he told me we might not see each other again. I said, "No Father, don't worry. We will see each other again."

In April 1991 I received a letter, followed by a phone call, from my wife saying that my father was seriously ill and that I should fly home. I told her I would be home as quickly as possible, though it is 18,000 miles from here. I started preparations. I was to fly to India at 11 o'clock at night. In the morning, I left as usual for my office in San Jose. It had been my routine since November 1989 to go to the temple on my way to work. I had to turn right on to a side street from Mission to go to the temple. It was about 6.25 to 6.30 a.m. when I made my right turn. Suddenly, for a few moments I passed out, or what I do not know. The car went into the flower bed on the right side of the street. There was just room enough for the car width in the flower bed or it would have scratched against the wall next to it.

'I drove right through the flower bed for about 15 to 20 yards and pulled out to the main street. The temple was near by. I parked, got out of the car and looked around for damage. The right side of the bumper was slightly dented. I kept on wondering for what earthly reason this should happen. In the evening I flew to India. After about 24 hours I reached home. When my van stopped in front of my home, none of my children or family members came out. I was shocked to learn the dreadful news of my surrogate father's death and cremation the previous day. After settling at home I started talking about the time of his death. I was even more shocked to learn that the time of my father's death was when my car bumped off the road.'

The existence of the psychic adoptive link is good news for all those families where step-parents, foster children and unrelated people of different generations share a household. It is possible for warm, intuitive connections to develop that confirm that love is not dependent solely on DNA strands.

However, alongside the natural and justifiable wish adopted children have to contact their birth parents, there can sometimes be untold hurt to adoptive parents, who have given years of love and devotion. Love is not mutually exclusive, and it is possible for an adopted adult to have close relationships with birth parents and the adopted family, as Linda and Dick have encouraged for Ivan. However, it is difficult for adoptive parents when an adult child rediscovers his or her birth family, and much more help is needed in this most delicate of all situations. Family bonds are not without pain.

# 10

---

# PSYCHIC GENERATIONS

F or some families, psychic contact is a way of life and is
accepted as an alternative or even an extra channel of
communication. Relations who have died are regarded as
absent rather than gone for ever. The sudden presence of a
dead gran's perfume or grandad's favourite pipe tobacco are
signs he or she has just popped by as they might have
done in life.

One explanation for this added dimension to family life is
that some families pass psychic gifts from generation to
generation. From an early age, children may take it for granted that aunty will turn her teacup upside down and see what
is in store. Often sensible advice is included in the prophecy.
Or mum may warn one of the teenagers not to take his motorbike out on a particular night. Some psychic families do not
have long histories, but discover their intuitive abilities and
sixth sense after a spontaneous psychic experience, that may
be triggered by a bereavement or reversal in worldly
fortunes.

My own theory is that whether they are first or sixth-
generation psychics, families where sixth-sense information
is accepted and used in a positive way are often those where
there is an open approach to life and a willingness to listen to

new ideas and opinions. Whether there are members of the family who use their intuitive abilities professionally, or automatically as a part of the everyday world, the psychic family can be found in the most down-to-earth settings. Lilian lives in a semi in the new town of Bracknell, and is a third-generation clairvoyant. She was brought up from early childhood with two psychic grandmothers and a mother and father with the gift of second-sight.

Now people come to her for help and advice, a tarot or a crystal ball reading, just as they did to her mother and grandmothers, when more conventional methods of coping with the world fail.

Unlike some of the people I have encountered, who were disbelieved or punished when they spoke of seeing ghosts or foretold the future, Lilian was brought up in an atmosphere that happily accepted the supernatural without leaning to the extremes of the occult. At one stage of her childhood Lilian was a very strong Christian, and this faith co-existed quite happily with her other beliefs.

Lilian was born in 1937, and when she was two the family moved from Manchester to a little village in Cheshire:

'The cottage had a thatched roof and dirt floor. I can remember Dad laying a proper one. It was called Holly Cottage. There was a pump outside and a stone two feet high on the floor by the fireplace.'

The cottage was built around the stone, and when Lilian visited the cottage years later she saw that, although her former home had been modernised and the thatch was gone, the stone in the centre was still there. Lilian always thought of it as a magic stone in her childhood.

One of her first memories was of an invisible friend, an ancient Egyptian girl, though she can't remember her name. Her mum told her in later years that Lilian was about three years old when the Egyptian girl came into their lives:

'The Egyptian girl was very close to me, like a sister. She said you had to wear your plaits in front of the shoulders to denote rank. I can still recall the place she used to take me, the tall rushes and water and beautiful flowers growing on top of the water, like water lilies but prettier.'

Her mother recalled how Lilian used to come out with all

sorts of information about Ancient Egypt that she could not possibly have known at that age. But as Lilian grew older, her invisible friend faded.

During the Blitz Lilian's grannies moved in with her family. They both read the teacups, and Lilian's house became the place for local people to go to seek the future:

'Granny Burton, Dad's mother, was Irish and read the cards as well as the teacups. She was a powerful woman, but very pretty, with her white hair streaked with golden strands. Granny Leonard was tiny, very prim and proper, with aspirations to being middle-class.'

Lilian's mother had a psychic talent that was not as conventional but nonetheless useful:

'Ma had the gift for finding gold. If there was a line of dustbins, she would know if one of them had anything gold in, and I would be sent to forage. Ma was very interested in rubbish dumps. She would tell me where to look, and sure enough there would be a bit of lost jewellery or a nice ornament. She'd point and say, "Look just there and see what's under the pile."

'I went through a phase of intense embarrassment when I was in my early teens, and would dodge out of Ma's dowsing trips.

'When I was little, I used to show off at tea-leaf reading sessions, and by three or four years old had developed my own clientele. "Let the little one do the reading," people used to say.'

Both the grandmas were strong believers in rules for the reading of the teacups, and Lilian was made to learn and obey them.

Rule 1. Do not acknowledge people to whom you've given readings when you meet them on the street, unless they speak first.

Rule 2. Try not to see anything unavoidably bad, and do not worry the clients. (Lilian says the conditioning of Granny Leonard and Burton was so strong she didn't see anything bad – and still doesn't).

Rule 3. If you see anything avoidably bad, try to see how it can be averted for your client.

Granny Burton used to watch Lilian reading the cups and

ask, "Where did you see that, child?"

When Lilian showed her, Granny Burton would poke at the leaves with her fingers and then say, "Carry on, child."

Lilian recalled that all was not sweetness and light:

'The grannies didn't really approve of each other. The problem was that they both knew they were right all the time. Grandad Leonard used to take me out for walks while they were sorting out their differences. He was interested in herbs and a natural herbalist, though he had been a master carpenter by trade.

'I went to a local school for a while, but didn't like it as it was so dull. So I changed to another village school right opposite the church. The local vicar was very nice to me and took a marked interest in me, perhaps because of the family reputation with the tea leaves.'

Following the family tradition, Lilian began casting love spells of her own in the playground from about the age of five:

'One of the children would say, "Do a spell," and immediately I would create one. At that time love was in short supply. The war was on and parents were very busy, often with dads away fighting.

'I always had a gift for poetry, so I found it very easy to make up a song or a chorus and get the other children in the playground to dance in and out in a chain dance. Then I would throw the wish into the middle. Sometimes the petitioner stood in the middle as well. I think my love spells always worked because people wanted them to.'

The spells gave Lilian confidence at school and made her very popular. Perhaps because the local clergy spent a lot of time with her, she became very much a Christian. She had been told by a teacher or the vicar that sometimes Satan tempted people, so you had to say, "Get thee behind me, Satan," and this obviously fired her imagination:

'As I was walking to school I used to be tempted by a cheeky, little devil, complete with a little forked tail. I used to hit him away behind me, over my shoulder. When I was with someone and the devil appeared, I used to have to slip off somewhere private and hit him back.

'Granny Leonard communicated with the spirits, and she was convinced the spirits sent her omens and signs understandable only to herself. She once told me: "I saw a man with a wooden leg yesterday –he was on the right-hand side of the road and crossed the road in front of me 20 paces before I reached him," and "There's a man in a brown hat, who crossed over on to the left side of the road."

'Granny Leonard would become still and adopt her significant expression. If I asked her, "What do you mean?", she would become even more mysterious, look very smug, and inform me, "You're too young to know." To this day I still do not know the significance of a man with a wooden leg crossing over the road, but I know it is not a good omen!'

Lilian's father was a fireman. 'He was a very good climber. He had gone to Australia during the Depression, and worked in a circus as a trapeze artist. He would be sent during the war to get German parachutists out of trees. He was against the family tea leaf readings though he was psychic himself. Dad had an amazing knack of seeing if someone was going to die, even if they were not ill.

'While in hospital on several occasions for stomach operations, he really came into his own. He would point to some chap in the ward and say to Mam, "He's away", and sure enough the man would be in the morgue before the day was out. Eventually the nurses told my mother, " Give us the nudge if he mentions anyone."'

When Lilian was nearly seven she got a shadow on her lungs and had well over a year off school. She had whooping cough and scarlet fever, and was taken to see a specialist in Chester, whose only treatment was that she should be allowed to live outdoors as much as possible.

'I ran wild. I was left to my own devices and started to see things in a different way. I got very close to nature and began to be aware of presences. The grans had settled back in Manchester after the war, so they only came on visits. But I used to discuss the presences with my mother.

'I started to learn to use my willpower to bring about the people living in the plants and flowers I found growing in the countryside. I found myself looking at the little people in shadowy forms. I watched them, but didn't really talk to them.

I was aware even then that other people did not have the time to see them. I used to tell Mum about them, but Dad didn't want to know.'

Lilian should have been learning to read and write and do arithmetic, but she thinks this lack of formal education gave her time for the other areas of her brain to develop.

When she was 14, Lilian won a scholarship to a school of art. 'I realised that I had to be careful, not put myself in the line of ridicule, so I played down my psychic abilities. It was a real culture shock to go to art college. For a time I forgot about doing spells, seeing that other people couldn't do them.'

Somewhere about his time she was introduced to the tarot cards, and took to them straight away. She had always read ordinary cards, as taught by Granny Burton, so this was just one step on from that – 'Tarot readings were considered more permissible in college society.'

At the age of 17, Lilian came south, determined not to let anyone know she was psychic. 'I would just be an ordinary person and not let on about my powers. But I found that complete strangers at odd times somehow guessed I knew things and could make predictions.'

Lilian married young, and by 19 had her first child. She gave the odd reading during this time, and gradually built up a clientele.

For many mothers the birth of their children establishes a psychic link that they had not suspected could exist. But Lilian, for all her intuitive skills, found herself as nervous as any other first-time mother:

'My eldest child completely blew my brains. I was so desperate to be a perfect mum, I ignored my psyche. I used to get up every hour during the night and hold a glass in front of my daughter's face to see if she was still breathing. By the second child, I'd got my act together. If Peg was restless, I could send thoughts to calm her down. With the younger ones I could send thoughts to the cot or pram from wherever I was round the house to stop them crying.'

How did Lilian's children feel about growing up with a psychic mother? Lesley, Lilian's youngest daughter, is the one who has followed most closely in her mother's psychic footsteps. Lesley is an artist by profession. At weekends, she can be found telling fortunes at fetes and fairs, casting the runes and reading the tarot cards.

Lilian's children were, like her, brought up in the countryside. Lesley told me:

'It was really beautiful where we lived, and we children used the countryside as our garden. It seemed very magical. We lived in an old house at a crossroads. There was a deserted lane and a big mansion that used to be a sanatorium. We used to play in the garden. We used to call it the Japanese or magic garden. There was a magical lake, and we used to run inside the empty house. We had lots of bird friends and used to talk to them.

'When it was sunset we used to hear the drummer in the sky beating the drums, and we knew it was time to go home. The sunset would come up and we had to get home before the sunset went over our heads or we'd be goners. We would run down the little hill like billy-o.

'We used to see misty figures, and Peg often saw ghosts. There was a house down the road that was haunted. Peg stayed in her friend's bedroom and once woke to see a blue lady sitting on the bed drinking a blue cup of tea. Another time, in the same bedroom, Peg looked up and saw a man in a turban with a sword, waving it above her head. Peg was about eight at the time and I was a year younger.

'Another time, Peg came dashing into our house to tell me to come and see the ghosts. There were two pillars we used to climb on, which marked the entrance where a big gate once was. There were four ghosts sitting on the pillars. They were four children.'

Lesley's interest in runes began in her childhood. 'When I was young I used to throw stones and twigs, and made amulets and charms with them. Everything was a ritual. I used to see the past and future with the runes I made. I made up my own meanings for the symbols I put on them. I could tell who a person's family were before I knew them, and could always see their parents. I would sometimes read my runes for friends and family, but mainly preferred to play with them by myself. I used to feel stones, and knew them to be magic and powerful. You have to let the ability develop naturally.'

Lesley says she could tell the future, but in the family tradition would not foretell doom, only give warnings. 'I did not realise I was brought up differently from other kids until I was about 25 . Mum was very in tune with the universal laws. She did spells at home. I didn't meet many people as a child because we lived in the country, so I didn't realise Mum was different.

'Lesley's friends would come to her for tarot readings, which she had been doing since the age of about eight. She also helped people with the zodiac.

'When Mum stepped into school on open nights, some of the girls were quite scared of her. Her blonde hair was fluffed out and she would wear flowing dresses with huge medieval sleeves. She used to waltz into school. People would say, "Wow, is that your mother?"' One woman used to cross herself when she passed our house.

'People were always coming to Mum for sessions of clairvoyance, and to ask her advice. She was a sort of little psychic Claire Rayner. My mother was helpful in a different way from the orthodox. It was easier to go to someone on the fringes of society. People would come knocking on the door for tea leaf readings or healing.

'Mum used to dance round the flowers, but it was a private thing to her. I used to look out of the window late at night sometimes and see her cavorting round the bushes in the moonlight. She would do spells at the new moon. But they were always harmless ones, to make good things happen.

'We would sing songs and go on adventures together with Mum, jumping over streams, picking flowers and eating fresh herbs.

'I suppose Mum was far from perfect at a mundane level. But she was very into spiritual things, and she was very positive and encouraging and mine was a good childhood.'

Lesley describes her own son as very gifted and creative, with tremendous insight. But it is George, Peg's son, who seems to be pursuing the more direct psychic line, according to his gran and his Aunty Lesley. He calls himself the spirit warrior (the name of a rune symbolising bravery, which Lesley used to think was her own).

He lives only a few doors away from Lesley's house, which is where I met him. He was eager to tell me about his runes, which he made himself. "I found the stones on the floor and put marks on them." His aunt and granny told me he used to throw his runes to see if he was going to have a good day at school.

Will George turn his back on the psychic world as he grows up, when many men do seem to find it hard to incorporate the occult into their lives in the way that women do? Or will George go on to develop his abilities and carry them on to the sixth generation?

There was nothing secret about Lilian's world, and while some psychologists may disapprove of a childhood removed from the mainstream, growing up in a world where nature is a part and material goods a secondary consideration may be no bad thing.

Lilian and Lesley have used their psychic gifts professionally. Sometimes the result of a psychic childhood is less direct. Dave Barrett is a TV and radio presenter, who appears on HTV and Radio Bristol. He is known for his interest in all kinds of psychic phenomena, not surprising since he has Romany roots. His family trusts and openly acknowledges their intuitive links and abilities.

Dave's psychic past has helped him to be open and sympathetic to people with all kinds of problems, and to tune into their underlying worries. He himself uses the tarot to make decisions. Dave's mother spoke to me:

'Our first joint family experience was when Dave was about six and the family were living in Slough. The family house was inside a big park. One evening we were in the garden as twilight was falling. Six huge cigar-shaped objects, black with a reddish tinge, came over in formation. They were not planes as we were used to seeing those, since we lived so near to Heathrow. Nor were they balloons of any kind, or airships. My husband, uncle, Dave and I all saw them quite clearly, and have never before or since seen anything like them. They were glowing, and though the moment seemed to last for ever it was fleeting, and then they were suddenly gone. We were convinced we had seen UFOs. My uncle was so excited he went out and bought a huge telescope. We spent hours in the garden tracking but never saw them again.

'My grandmother and grandfather were Romanies. They

bought and trained horses for the Army, and my grandma used to ride them bareback. My grandfather worked as a wheelwright for the Army. Sadly my granny died when she was quite young. She was only 48. The family came originally from Hungary. My father used to speak Romany but refused to teach it to us. I remember once hearing him praying in Romany when he thought we could not hear. My granny used to smoke a clay pipe but like all her Romany world, it was kept hidden from us, as my father wanted us to grow up like the children around.

'But there were differences between our family and others. Aunty Leila, my father's aunt, owned a lot of property, including a beautiful bungalow. She would never live in a house, only in a caravan. When she died her caravan was burned according to tradition, so that her spirit would be free.

'The family would never allow any white china or china ornaments in their homes in case it brought illness. They would have nothing to do with fortune telling, and refused even to read the teacups for other people, although they always knew when someone would die or something happen.

'My mother was not psychic or did not show it, although I had many spirit friends when I was a child. I am very close to Dave and invariably when I go to pick up the phone to dial him he will say, "Hello, mum" as he has just dialled my number. I know even now he is grown up and has his own home, if he is ill or in pain or even worried. I will wake in the night and sense he is not well, just as I used to when he was a child. He knows if I am having an achy day or a muggy head, because he has one too. I can sense if he is in danger.

'The most startling premonition was one both Dave and I shared but neither of us acted on. Dave was due to do a personal appearance in a Bristol club one Friday evening. I had a dreadful feeling that something would happen to him if he went. I did not say anything because I did not want to seem as if I was fussing or interfering in his life.

'Unknown to me, Dave was also very worried about going that evening, as he felt that he would be attacked, stabbed and killed. Dave almost cancelled the date, but because of all the advance publicity he felt he should not let the club down.

Dave got into the car still feeling very edgy. It was a nasty, icy night. As Dave's car was going round a bend, although he was driving very slowly, it skidded into a lamp-post. The car was a total write-off, but Dave fortunately was just badly bruised. All evening I had felt restless and worried. It was a relief when the phone call came to say that Dave had survived.

We both felt that something dreadful would have happened if Dave had reached the club. Dave is convinced he would have been stabbed to death and that fate had caused the car to go off the road to save his life.

'If I feel uneasy now I always tell him and he listens. My husband calls me an old witch.'

Not all psychic families stretch back generations. And few go on to use their psychic gifts in the working world, although they are usually sympathetic people to whom others turn naturally and share their troubles. It may be that a significant family event acts as a catalyst for existing but unacknowledged or undeveloped powers.

Take Jo's family. Unusually it was the men who began the psychic chain. Jo lives in Berkshire and has a good job in a media company. Jo's father, Ron, is a medium, although it is only since the death of his own father that he has developed his powers. An inexplicable family experience confirmed for Ron that there was something beyond the material world.

Jo explained: 'After my grandfather died eight years ago, Dad was driving his Range-Rover. Suddenly his father was there, telling him urgently, "Get out of the car now!"

'Dad pulled over to the side of the road and got out. Seconds later the dashboard exploded. Since then he was been aware that my grandfather is with him, protecting him.

'I have only known for about four years that my father was developing his psychic abilities. Until then he kept very quiet about it, only telling Mum. One night the whole family was in the kitchen and Dad was getting ready to go out. My father does a lot of charity work and was finding it hard to find the time to go to his development circle. Dad told us he was going to give mediumship up and concentrate on the real world. He went to change and I followed him up the stairs. Suddenly there was an overwhelming smell of pungent lavender.

'My grandfather loved lavender and used to pick it off any bushes he saw, crush the flowers and put them in his pocket. Mum, Dad, my sister Kate and I could smell lavender for about five minutes, until Dad said he would carry on with the circle. The strong scent disappeared and Dad is convinced it was his father's way of telling him not to give up.

'Grandad was the most spiritual man I knew and yet he always insisted that "When you're gone, you're gone." I've got a tape of him talking to me when I was five. On it he's saying I shouldn't be afraid of ghosts because they don't exist. However, Grandad always knew when my dad was in trouble and would go to him. When Dad was in his teens he went on a camping trip with two of his mates and didn't tell anyone where they were staying. The lads were a long way from home, where they hadn't been before, and everything went wrong. They were totally rained out and were cold, hungry and fed up. At that moment my grandad turned up in the field to take them home. He just knew where his son was.

'Another time Dad had gone to an older friend's house, and things got out of hand. Again he hadn't told his father where he was going, but his father turned up to sort things out at the crucial moment. Again Grandad tuned in.

'When Dad ignored Grandad's warnings things went very wrong. One particular day Grandad told my father not to go round a certain corner on his motorbike or he would fall off and get hurt. Dad wouldn't listen. The same evening he did ride round the corner Grandad warned him against, and my father was involved in an accident. He ended up in hospital, having injured his knees badly.

'I was very close to my grandad and linked into his death, though we were on holiday in the south of France and he was in Harrow. I was 13 at the time. I woke late in the evening and experienced the most terrible palpitations and chest pains. The pains were so bad I thought I was dying. Then they were gone and I went straight back to sleep.

'The next morning a neighbour of my grandfather phoned to say he had suddenly died of a heart attack at 11 p.m. Given the time difference, that was when I had experienced the chest pains.'

The most psychic member of the family is Kate, Jo's 19-

year-old Down's syndrome sister. Over the years I have come across many psychic experiences involving Down's syndrome children. Perhaps because the left, logical side of the brain develops more slowly, the Down's syndrome child has an easier access to spirituality. Jo explained:

'My Dad's spirit guide is a Red Indian. There was a black cat who came regularly to our door and we used to give him food. Kate took an instant dislike to that cat and said, "Don't let the cat in. He is a Red Indian spirit cat."

'Recently Mum, Dad and Kate went on holiday to Scotland, and as they were driving across Culloden Moor Kate said, "I can see people on that field with their heads cut off."

Kate knew nothing of the history of the place.

'Dad felt an impulse to go back to Culloden, and he and Mum went for a walk up a steep hillside. Dad found the way barred by a big Scotsman who said, "All who pass, pass by me," and disappeared. Mum said Kate had put the spooks up them because she doesn't like walking. They didn't go on.

'Kate has had an invisible friend called Michael for over two years. He is not like an imaginary friend where you have to lay a place at the table for him. Michael is only in Kate's bedroom, and there are strange conversations with him where she waits for an answer. Kate tells us that only she can see him, and clams up if we ask questions about him. Of course, she is very cunning and will use Michael as an excuse if she doesn't want us to go in her room. But even that is strange.

'When my parents and Kate were on holiday recently, my boyfriend and I stayed at the house to take care of it. It is a big, friendly house with a lovely atmosphere, but we sensed the whole time that something was missing. We both felt frightened and could not go into Kate's room while she was away. I felt that Michael was in there. Kate had told me Michael would be looking after her room, so I couldn't go in. But both of us couldn't even walk on the landing outside. The moment Kate and my father walked through the door it was as if the house breathed a sigh of relief and the atmosphere was right again.'

So is Michael a spirit friend or an imaginary one? Jo told me that two and a half years ago, about the time Michael appeared in the house, her father was in hospital for a back operation. While Ron was there, he started to write what he believes was spirit-inspired poetry, and certainly he had never written poetry before. The strangest poem was one called, 'Mike Behind the Door', about a boy called Michael who was crippled by spina bifida and was confined to a room in a home. Because he could not walk. Michael saw life only from behind the door and his view of the world was the central heating pipes of the radiator above him.

'Soon after my father wrote that poem, Michael began to live in Kate's room and could not or would not come out. When the family asked Kate if Michael had hurt legs or was better, Kate acted very strangely and totally clammed up.'

Jo's grandfather triggered off the family psychic life by his death. Many families do have psychic experiences over more than one generation. As a society, we do not encourage the telling of such stories, and so it is often a hidden aspect of family life. Often women find it easier to recount such experiences, and even today men, especially in Britain, are too often expected to be logical and keep a stiff upper lip.

Lilian, Dave and Jo are all happy, successful people who have an added dimension to their lives, because psychic communication is a natural part of family experience. All trust and use their sixth-sense quite spontaneously. This enables them to anticipate hazards and see beyond the immediate. Psychic families are generally positive units where family members are not bound by guilt and obligation. Why then should psychologists be so wary of the psychic family? In the next chapter I look at families where the psychic is used in a negative way, and examine dark psychic experiences that occur when family tensions are repressed and unresolved.

# 11

# FAMILY SECRETS

M argaret, who lives in Scotland, also had a long family tradition of brushes with the paranormal. For her, however, these other-world encounters were frightening until she understood them. Margaret's great-grandmother began the family tradition, and Margaret's mother had psychic experiences in her own childhood that continued into adult life.

However, Margaret felt very isolated with her own childhood ghosts. Many parents who see or feel a ghost next to their child, fear that if they acknowledge the presence, their child may be even more terrified. The reverse tends to be true, and a child or adult left alone with a haunting only he or she apparently witnesses, can feel threatened or even worried they are going mad.

'My maternal great-granny had second-sight and read the cards. There are quite a few stories about her foretelling funerals of local people.

'My mother remembers one morning walking with her granny. Suddenly her granny told her to come to the side of the road because the funeral of Jed, a local man, was passing by. Mum could see no one. Shortly afterwards, Jed did die suddenly. His funeral passed by that spot a week later, at the time the old lady had seen it.

'My mother, great-grandma's only child's youngest child, had her first experience when she was very small. Mum was unable to sleep because she could hear breathing. My great-gran was in the house at the time. No one else could hear the breathing. My grandma was cross that my mum was being silly but my great-granny told my gran not to scold my mother as she had inherited the gift. Finally the breathing stopped. A neighbour came to fetch my grandfather, five or ten minutes later, as a family member had died at the moment that my mother ceased to hear the breathing.

'My mother's granny taught her to read the playing cards. However, my mother stopped doing it when she saw that a friend's father would be killed in an accident. It happened shortly afterwards. On several occasions my mother has heard a bump or bang and my father has had a minor car accident at that moment. Mother has continued to have these experiences throughout her life.

'She saw my late uncle, her brother John, in her bedroom mirror in 1977. Mum was putting clothes away in a dressing table. She looked up and saw him, He had a sombre expression. When she said, "Johnny," and turned round to touch him, he had gone. They had always been very close, and Uncle Johnny's death in 1972 was a big blow to her as it was very sudden.

'About six months later, our family moved to a farm cottage in the country. Here I had my first memorable but terrifying experience. My bedroom was above my parents', and I was only seven at the time. I was only told my mother's part of the story two or three years later. The temperature in my room would drop very suddenly, and on several occasions my mother would be in bed at night, hear footsteps above and think I was awake. She would come upstairs and find me fast asleep. My father heard nothing.

'The strange thing was one night Mum heard the footsteps and shook my father awake. While she was touching him, Dad could hear the footsteps. When she let go of him he could not.

'Another night Mum awoke to hear me screaming. She rushed upstairs. Halfway up it was as if she had met a wall of cold air, so strong it seemed almost solid. I had often had this feeling in my bedroom. Mum came into my room and it was freezing. She asked me what was wrong. I was very upset and crying out that someone was looking at me. I was pointing behind her to where the presence was. I seem to be able to feel presences in houses, and on two occasions my mum has been with me when this happened. I can just feel it somehow, a horrible sensation.

'My mum made enquiries after we moved out of the cottage. A family had lived there in the 1940s whose daughter's first name and surname coincidentally was the same as mine, and she had also had disturbed nights in my room.

'Strange noises had been heard, and at last her parents had lifted the floorboards of their room, that was directly below hers. Bones were found, and the local minister said they should be reburied in that spot. When we checked local history, a battle had taken place nearby between the McRaes, the Macdonalds and the Frasers, from all three of whom I am descended on my mother's side.

'Until I was 17, I regularly heard someone calling me. When I went to my mother, she would tell me she had not spoken at all. I went to see a gypsy woman at a fair and she told me that a close family member on my mother's side, a woman, was watching over me. My psychic ability had come down through her. This woman had wanted me to have a treasure of hers, but it was broken. Therefore it had not been given to me. There was a special picture of this woman surrounded by flowers. The gypsy told me this was the woman who was calling me.

'I was upset, and I told my mother the gypsy's words. Mum gave me a necklace her mother had worn that Gran had wanted me to have when she died. The pendant part was broken, and so my mother had not passed it on. Inside the pendant was a picture of my granny (whom I resemble) in a garden surrounded by flowers.

'Over the years I hear the voice less and less. My mum has told me not to be afraid of feeling, hearing or seeing things as it is quite natural.'

Margaret was afraid until she discovered that the voice she heard was her grandma guiding her, rather than a malevolent force. Because Margaret has a good relationship with her mother, the psychic family tradition has at last become an ability to be accepted openly by them both, and used not feared. Margaret's account demonstrates how important it is to talk through and share psychic experiences good and bad.

In contrast, my own psychic family life was hidden and, unlike the accounts of the families in the last chapter, was based on fear and secrecy. My father was excluded from the early experiences, although his own family had grown up on the canals and so had a rich folklore.

Perhaps this is why the early experiences I had were largely negative. When I was a young teenager, my family rented a cottage in Anglesey. There was a very old, dark antique shop my mother and I visited to buy old books, my mother's hobby. Though we lived in a cramped terraced house in the back streets of Birmingham and my dad worked in a factory, my mother was determined we should have a proper library in the front room. In Anglesey we bought two ancient leather family Bibles, an obscure Latin book and ten miniature volumes of *History of England*, that I always believed would be the key to great riches, since they were reputedly the only copy in the world.

It was the Bibles that caused the trouble. The cottage, on a remote hillside, was very old and had an atmosphere of evil and decay. That afternoon, as the Bibles lay on the table, the biggest spider I have ever seen ran across them and refused to be driven away.

In the morning the Bibles were covered with webs and deep scratches. My mother hung her crucifix over them, but each night more webs and scratches would appear. This knowledge was kept between my mother and myself.

A year later, my mother began to develop a friendship with a neighbour's husband, who was a builder and was employed to modernise our house. I felt very resentful of the growing warmth and laughter between them. At Easter my mother and I took a day trip to Weston-super-Mare. We were walking through the back streets when my mother saw a dingy shop offering the services of 'Madame Smythe, Clairvoyant and Crystal Ball Reader'. I was left in a dusty outer room while my mother went behind the fraying velvet curtain with an old woman with yellowed, rotting teeth and straggling grey hair tied back in a red silk scarf. Madame Smythe wore huge gold dangling earrings. I branded her a fraud, annoyed because the curtain was too thick to allow me to eavesdrop. When my mother came out about half an hour later, she was crying and had lost interest in our day out. We caught the train home almost immediately. I never knew exactly what Madame Smythe imparted, except that my mother was in love with a man whose initial was 'P' – the builder's name was Pete – and that my mother had great psychic gifts. For the first time my mother excluded me from her world, which now seemed bound up with Pete.

Harmless pandering to the romantic nature of an obviously unhappily married middle-aged woman, who otherwise would not have had a lot to look forward to? However, Madame Smythe's clairvoyance changed my mother's life in a more sinister way. My mother began to receive messages from the late George V1 and also her own father. She would write, apparently automatically, messages of great importance. Gradually her writing at such times became totally unreadable except to her, but the contacts increased, and soon she heard voices constantly in her head that would not leave her alone even at night.

From irritated amusement at her brush with deceased royalty, I became terrified and totally unable to offer any help. My mother seemed to withdraw almost entirely from reality. My father was not told, and so far as I know he had not the slightest awareness of the reason for the change in my mother. Perhaps he found she was easier to live with.

When the voices would not let her rest day or night, even she became afraid. At last she confided in her parish priest, who did not mock her but said he had seen terrible examples of possession during his time as a chaplain at sea. Mum went to the church to be exorcised. During the ceremony a hideous old man apparently ran up and down the aisle screaming obscenities. Whether he was real or not I do not know.

Afterwards the experiences stopped totally, and the paranormal was not discussed again in our household. But our underlying love, chained to possessiveness, continued over the years and my mother told me, "If you leave me I shall die."

I went away to college in spite of this, and shortly afterwards my mother became terminally ill. Though I was only 19, I nursed her through cancer, but she died blaming me for her illness because I had left her alone in an unhappy marriage.

However, we shared some close, happy moments at the end. On the last evening she was more alert than usual. She hovered between total lucidity and hallucination. Then she asked me if we were allowed to make scrambled eggs. I cooked supper, which unusually she ate with enthusiasm. I washed her and sat by her bedside in our front room, watching the embers of a bonfire on the waste ground opposite. Suddenly her face was transformed from the yellowing, papery, ravaged face of the last weeks with a golden glow. "George", she said, and my blood froze as I recalled her previous experiences. To my relief I realised she was talking to her dad, Albert George, at least I have to believe she was. "You've come for me," she said, and for the first time we both slept peacefully.

Early the next morning she died. Because I didn't know that people could return, I wasn't able to use what might have been very healing experiences to come to terms with her loss and the accompanying guilt.

After her death, I began to see her in the night, sitting by my bedside wearing her old brown mac and looking as she did before her illness. We would be talking about my day as a student teacher, and she would say, "Go and put the kettle on, Bab".

I knew she was dead and that she must not be there. Her voice would fade away as it did in her last moments. I was terribly afraid to go to sleep. Now I can see she was perhaps trying to make things right.

I would often see my mother in the daytime too, sitting on the bench at the bus stop opposite. I never went over, and stopped looking out of the window. I feared what I did not understand, and went to my doctor for help.

My GP, an elderly traditionalist, gave me tranquillisers, and the visitations stopped. I suppressed all thoughts of my mother quite consciously, and if anyone mentioned her I would change the subject. This continued for two years, and was my way of coping. It is only since I have been a mother myself that I have understood some of the pressures that made her so possessive towards me.

Although I knew on a logical basis that I was in no way responsible for her death, deep down I still felt guilty. Twenty-five years later I was writing a book about resolving guilt with family members who have died. One night I had a dream that seemed more than a dream. I was preparing to pack to go away to college, although I was no longer young. My mother was helping and she asked me, "Will you be home this weekend, Bab?"

"No, Mom. It's too far and I've got my own life to live now," I replied.

"That's all right. You must not worry about me. I shall be fine."

My mother had finally let me go. Whether psychic or psychological, the dream was immensely healing. Could it have been wishful thinking, I have been asked. I can't repeat the experience under laboratory conditions. I can't produce witnesses. Although I briefly told the story in *Families are Forever*, I did not acknowledge the experience as my own. It was not until an article on the book was published and a reporter asked whether I had seen any family ghosts, that I realised my story might be of interest to other people. Since then I have told this tale in America as well as Britain, and found that many people not only understood but had similar unresolved guilt.

With my first two children, I did not recognise any psychic experiences, which is not the same as saying they did not have any. As I said in the Introduction, when Jack was two and a half he told me that his dad had gone 'roly-poly' on his motorbike, but was all right. That single inexplicable incident changed my whole view, not to mention launching me on a career I frequently intend to quit, but never get the time.

Since then my younger children have reported many strange incidents. It may be they feel more comfortable sharing their rich inner world, because I no longer automatically dismiss their insights as fantasy. I no longer see my mother, even in dreams. My younger daughter Miranda frequently sees Granny Beryl sitting on her bed. Granny Beryl often tells her stories, and the relationship is a positive one. I was surprised when Miranda commented after a television programme on which I had appeared that my hair was exactly like Granny Beryl's. On special occasions, my mother would wear her hair on top in a French pleat. This particular show was, however, the only time I had ever worn my hair that way – the work of an ingenious make-up girl – to calm my unruly curls. There are no photos of my mother with her hair piled up.

Miranda is also visited by my late Aunt Ruth, my mother's sister, who lived with me as a child. Ruth was always very fond of Miranda, whom I think, reminded her of me as a child. One night my aunt appeared in Miranda's bedroom in her wheelchair – Miranda describes her as a picture on the wall. She told Miranda, "I'm all right now, dearie."

The next day we heard she had died.

This is very different from my negative experience of an old lady who haunted me as a child. She would appear at the top of the stairs and drag me up. Then I felt myself floating and falling. The old lady lived in the cupboard in my room that contained all kinds of strange objects from the past – paper parasols and an old wedding veil with faded orange blossom. I knew the old lady hated me, and I went to sleep every night with my eyes transfixed on the cupboard. My own grandmother died in the house. She had hated children, especially her own, and would give my mother's and aunt's toys away while they were at school. Was it my granny I saw?

I suppose the real difference is that the silences and anger of my own childhood are replaced by a happier atmosphere with my own children, and the fact that we can talk about all experiences, including, but not specially psychic ones. When the paranormal takes its place as a part of, but not a focus of the family world, it loses its power to tie members together in unhealthy silence.

Family love, turned to hatred, can be devastating to those for whom the bond turns sour. For the telepathic channels of kinship give access to our very selves, in a way no stranger's curse can wound. Tony, from Hertfordshire, had an identical twin with whom he had a very close telepathic bond, until he became engaged to be married. It was the channel that Tony believes led him to suffer severe psychic attacks:

'In 1972 my brother John was lured into the Moonie cult, and has been a member ever since. I became very active in trying to get him out for several years, and during this time I experienced nasty spiritual attacks, usually during the early hours of the morning. On one occasion I was awakened from a deep sleep and quite suddenly a ball of fire some four feet across started rolling towards me from the foot of the bed.

'When it reached my chest it stopped, and in the fire was the face of my brother John. He was smiling and relaxed and told me, "Don't worry. Everything is going to be all right."

'As mysteriously as it had arrived, the ball of fire simply disappeared. At that time I had recently been converted to Christianity, and had been receiving regular counselling.

'I no longer have any contact with John, having been advised by my counsellor that to do so could leave me open to further spiritual attack. I still live in hope that one day he will be released from his bondage and we can resume our bond of love.'

Ruby, who lives in Los Angeles, also believes she was under psychic attack from her brother. She describes it as 'a ghost in my space that made me sick and gave me no rest.' These attacks seem to mirror the physical hatred Ruby's brother has:

'My brother has attacked me, intermittently, for years, surrounding me with hatred and evil. I have told him to leave me, and at last I have developed my own psychic and healing powers and he has gone. My brother is violent and has always hated me, and I blame him for my mother's death.

'Because of my brother, my mother and I were estranged for ten years. Yet I was always connected to her and knew she was around. Then one night I lost her. Mom was gone. I felt dizzy, had blurred vision, terrible stomach cramps and could not stop crying. I wrote to her begging her to let me know she was safe, as I knew she was in great danger.

'Seven days later she dropped dead. I was told the news by an attorney I did not know. My brother had not thought fit to inform me, though he was with her at the time. She was cremated within three days without my knowledge. For 30 days I was ill. I could see him in the corner. I saw evil creatures with him, black, white and grey, and I told him "William, I know it is you." I thought I would fall apart, and I prayed to God for a miracle to save me.'

Ruby has demonstrated that it is possible to overcome even such vicious attacks on the psyche. Some people seek help from a priest or healer, but others can develop personal ways of replacing darkness with positive thoughts and love. Fortunately such attacks are rare.

While I do not believe dark experiences and apparent poltergeist activity are always triggered by family tensions, in some cases an apparent haunting can perhaps be unconsciously fuelled by unresolved family business from the past. The relationship between psychological conflict and negative psychic energy is a complex one. Often hauntings do cease if anger or guilt in the home is resolved.

Belinda is in her late twenties and an assistant bank manager, definitely a lady on the fast track. The disturbances began when she moved into a flat in a smart north of England suburb. Though the building was new, her bedroom always felt freezing, no matter how high she turned up the heating. At night Belinda would wake to see a huge dark shadow standing over her bed, and a threatening voice telling her she would die.

Belinda had lived alone since leaving school, and tells me she is totally logical. Eventually the whisperings became intense, and the shadow would lean over and envelop her so she couldn't breathe. At last, reluctantly, Belinda decided to call in a spiritual healer. The healer carried out a blessing ceremony and told Belinda to visualise angels guarding her bed.

But she never felt comfortable in the flat, and soon afterwards sold it for another where she has experienced no problems.

Belinda told me that just before she moved into her new flat, she at last resolved a long-standing feud with her family over a child she had conceived as a schoolgirl and miscarried at a late stage. We don't know where the psychological ends and the psychic begins. It may be that certain places, such as Belinda's flat, do have potentially negative energies or presences that can be activated by unresolved anger or guilt. In the earlier chapter on adopted family ghosts, some accounts suggested that presences would not necessarily appear to every family who occupy a haunted house or flat. Whatever the source of the malevolence, an improvement in earthly affairs can only be an advantage.

Eileen, from Hampshire, had no bad psychic manifestations until one afternoon she went to bed feeling ill. She woke to find the room altered and totally black, although it was still daylight:

'I saw a small television set on an old wooden dresser, although I have neither a dresser nor a television in my bedroom. The pictures on the screen were dark grey. The moon hurtled up into the sky, a very dazzling silver, and then disappeared. Lightning, meteors and brilliant lights seemed to hurl themselves against the screen. Then the room altered and a woman was dusting the furniture, not saying anything or acknowledging me, but busy working, working, unable to rest as I was unable to rest. She appeared again that night, as did the TV screen, and every time I tried to sleep. I became ill and exhausted, haunted by the woman and these strange lights and noises.'

I went to see Eileen at her request, as she was afraid she was going mad. Although the bungalow she lived in was new, there was always the possibility that the land was haunted. There was a Catholic church and some very old houses near her home. Eileen's ghost had appeared suddenly, although Eileen had lived in the same place for several years. What had changed? I asked Eileen whether she had any worries, and she told me about a violent quarrel with her daughter-in-law the previous week. All contact was now cut with her son. There had been tension in the relationship from the beginning. Eileen had tried to ignore the mounting resentment on both sides, until bitter words of years of tension spilled out on both sides over an apparently trivial incident.

I suggested that Eileen might try to sort things out with the family, and she did. Order was restored and her ghosts never returned.

As worrying as psychic attack is an attempt to psychically control those we profess to love. Angela had been divorced for several years and had vowed never to remarry. However, she went along to a singles night, and was instantly drawn to a man who said he felt he had always known her. The old chat-up line proved true, as Guy seemed able to read Angela's thoughts and anticipate her needs as though they were an old married couple. After a short time Guy proposed and suggested she moved in with him. Angela felt incredibly drawn to Guy but was not ready to leave her home, and told him she wanted more time to get to know him.

Soon after, Angela started to wake very morning at 5 a.m. thinking of Guy, and was aware of his presence in the room, which would fade as soon as she was fully awake. At first Angela was flattered and amused, and thought that Guy must be dreaming of her.

Gradually, however, she found the early morning waking disturbing. Feeling foolish, Angela mentioned the experiences to Guy. He did not laugh, but told that he came to her every morning at 5 a.m. when he woke to go to work. He could even describe the nightdress she wore on a particular night, far too accurately for random guessing. Guy insisted that he wanted her to live with him, and would continue to come to her and contact her until she agreed. He told her he could get into her mind at any time.

When Guy's voice and image started appearing to Angela in her car as she drove on her rounds as a district nurse, Angela became afraid, and deliberately began blocking him out. However, she has continued the relationship. She half enjoys the struggle for telepathic control, but I am not certain that we should deliberately get into each other's minds or manipulate natural channels of communication. I fear that love may tip over into a power struggle.

Because the bonds of family are so powerful and intense, it is important that family members and close lovers do have emotional space and privacy that we do not try to invade psychically in order to change others' behaviour. This is very different from sending messages of love, or responding to an unspoken cry for help. Mind and soul games are dangerous.

Equally it is vital not to let hostility seethe away, or to allow our family, whether partner, parent or child, to manipulate use or destroy our self-esteem, physically or psychologically. Love can easily flip to hatred. If we do talk through, rather than deny negative feelings that appear in the most loving relationship, then love will remain predominant.

# 12

## OTHER DIMENSIONS

Out-of-Body Experiences and Near-Death Experiences are times when, if only for a moment, mortals leave the material plane. Although such incidents are well documented, the family connection is frequently overlooked. Yet this is perhaps the most exciting and reassuring aspect ,in personal terms, that we are still cared for by those we love, even when the rest of life temporarily fades.

Out-of-body experiences (OOBIEs) are usually entirely spontaneous, and prompted by emotion. They far outnumber deliberate attempts to travel astrally, which may be disappointing and sometimes even cause distress. A naturally occurring oobie involves rising above our physical form and sometimes seeing it below. The astral or etheric body has never been identified in experiments. Yet many people do believe that we each have a spirit shape that may rise to the ceiling and look down on the inert or sleeping earthly body, and on other family members. This form is said to pass through walls and doors, and even without effort or time passing, visit a family member who is many miles away. Usually the relation is ill, in distress or thinking very hard about a parent or partner. Most oobies have a reason.

Lucy's out-of-body experience happened many years ago,

when children of government officials were routinely sent from the colonies at a young age to boarding school in England. Before the days of fast, long-distance air travel, the children would be farmed out with relations during the holidays, and not return home for many years. Lucy was ten years old. Although she had been at school in England for two years, she was sitting in her dormitory one lunchtime crying because she was homesick, and some of the other girls had been teasing her.

Suddenly Lucy found herself above her body looking down at herself crouched on the bed. She remembers nothing except a sensation of rushing wind, a noise like an express train, and a feeling of being totally weightless. A moment later, she was in the huge, shaded family drawing room in India. Her ayah was arranging the blinds for the evening. Lucy ran to her, hugged her and burst into tears. Her nursemaid cuddled her, and at that moment Lucy's mother came into the room, wearing a lilac dress. Lucy also noticed there were new green tasselled and embossed covers on the chairs. The ayah pointed: 'Miss Lucy is here', she said, and for a moment Lucy says her mother looked at her and half moved towards her, before shaking her head.

At that moment a clock chimed. Lucy felt a rushing in her ears and re-entered her body with a bump. She was back in the dormitory, but was no longer so afraid and unhappy. She felt sure, against all logic, that her mother would come.

A telegraphed message came a few days later to say her mother would be coming for a visit to England the following month, and had taken a house in the local village so Lucy could be with her in the evenings and at weekends.

Lucy's mother was unusually attentive, and one evening Lucy confided in her about her strange experience. To her amazement, her mother did not dismiss it as imagination, but described how she had seen Lucy in the drawing room, although she denied it to the servant. Lucy's mother realised that her daughter needed her and decided to come, although she did not give Lucy's father the real reason. Lucy says he was a peppery military man who had no truck with what he called 'mumbo-jumbo'. Lucy's mother had been wearing a new lilac gown that day, and the covers on the chairs had been replaced by green brocade.

The story did not end entirely happily. Lucy explained to me that in those days, before the First World War, children were expected to be educated in England, so her mother returned to India without her, after settling the sale of her late father's paintings, the ostensible reason for the visit. In later years her mother could or would not recall the incident, and took the story to her grave without ever sharing it with her husband.

However, Lucy felt the experience, which she never forgot, showed that her mother loved her enough to cross the world to be with her, even for a short time. Lucy remembered those few weeks living with her mother as the happiest of her childhood.

Lucy was seen as a misty figure, although neither Lucy's nurse nor her mother thought she had died. However, living ghosts can appear hours or even days before that person does die. It is almost as if the spirit body begins to free itself from the body more frequently in preparation for death. Why should these pre-death visitations occur? Can strong thoughts of love, and perhaps a premonition that time may be short, prompt a grandfather to seek out a beloved grandchild? Gillian had always been very close to her grandfather:

'My grandad lived in London and I was in High Wycombe, visiting my boyfriend's house. I was staring out of the living room window. It was school holidays and children were playing football in the sunshine. On the corner was an elderly man dressed in a cap and with a mackintosh over his smart suit, just standing there.

'It seemed so odd as he was dressed for winter, and I realised that the children couldn't see him and were running through him. I turned to tell my boyfriend Phil that I was sure it was my grandad, but in that second he had vanished. I thought no more of it as the incident seemed so improbable. A week later my grandfather died unexpectedly and it all came together. It had been him, coming to say goodbye'.

There was no way Gillian's grandfather could physically have been in High Wycombe that day. The story, however, did not end there:

'On the day my grandfather died, he had gone off to his

part-time job as usual. My grandmother made his lunch about 12 o'clock. She told me she heard him come in, whistling as usual. He didn't come into the kitchen, and was nowhere to be found. Five minutes later, Grandad really did arrive, whistling. Again the door opened. Grandfather had not been home earlier, although my grandmother was convinced she had heard him. He went for a rest, and died shortly after.'

Near-death experiences occur when a person dies momentarily either during an operation or an accident. He or she may not only leave their body, although oobies are a part of this more intense phenomenon, but see lights, tunnels, hear beautiful music and even glimpse angels. Although such cases are well documented, what is often overlooked is that in almost every instance, a relation is waiting at the end of the dark tunnel. Whether a deceased grandmother, father or parent is seen, the presence of a relation gives an element of normality to a potentially frightening moment. The familiar presence offers reassurance and will send us home safely, as he or she did when we were a child.

Philip, who runs a car welding business in Southampton, had a near-death vision. As he passed briefly between life and death, he was greeted by his late grandmother:

'When I was on my honeymoon in Wells, my wife and I were walking through the bracken. I came across a snake. Wanting to show off, I picked it up. It was an adder and it bit me twice. I tried to suck the poison out, which made the situation worse as I swallowed the venom. So fast did the venom spread that I was unconscious by the time I got to hospital. I went into a dark tunnel towards a light. My grandmother, who had died eight years previously, was waiting for me, smiling and holding out her arms. She had been a Romany gypsy, and we had been very close when she was alive. I was pleased to see her again and hugged her. But she told me, "It is not your time. You must go back and finish your life."

I found myself back in my body in hospital in a room full of people, and later told my wife how I had seen my grandma. The experience was so vivid, I have never forgotten it'.

The following two experiences are in a sense two sides of the same coin. The first involves a father who had an out-of-body experience after the death of his wife. Gregory recalled:

'I was still comparatively young and very much in love with my wife. After five years of marriage she died from pneumonia. Although I tried to cope with the sorrow courageously, when I returned from the funeral I collapsed. I felt the cold pass up my body, and I was not afraid because I wanted to die too. I found myself with my wife on the other side.

'I argued with my wife that I wanted to stay with her. She was heartbroken to be separated from me. She told me that I must go back to look after the little ones, our baby daughter and our son. And so I did return. That was years ago, and the children are now grown up and married themselves.

But I have never forgotten the sorrow of coming back to the world.'

Sarah believes she chose to return to her husband rather than to stay on the other side with her baby daughter, who died at birth. It is easy, given the strength of the maternal bond, to forget the intensity of other family ties:

'When I was 36 I had a very difficult labour and was in great danger for my life. When I finally regained consciousness, the doctor was waiting beside my bed to tell me what I already knew. I had had a baby girl who had died very shortly after she was born.

"How do you know?" the doctor asked me.

'I explained I had a vision in which I was in a long white tunnel. At one end of it, my husband stood waiting for me. I was in the centre and a little girl stood at the other end, also waiting for me to go to her. A voice told me I had to decide whether I wanted to go to my husband or my baby, to live or to die. I chose to go back to my husband because he needed me so much, and it wasn't fair to leave him to grieve alone.'

Sarah's experience may seem strange, as she was giving birth when she had her near-death experience. Birth and death do not seem to belong together, and yet are two sides of the same coin. In my own research into this phenomena that has spanned several years, I have concluded that the near-birth experience mimics the near-death experience, but is entirely rooted in the mother/child link. Indeed, near-birth experiences, or NBEs as I call them, occur as a child is catapulted into this world, even when a mother or child's life is not in danger and no drugs have been administered.

Such birth experiences are not uncommon, and may vary from a moment of sheer bliss and oneness with the universe while giving birth, to a full-blown, lights, tunnels and angelic vision. Some mothers are able to glimpse another dimension as their baby enters this one. These birth visions are, I believe, rooted firmly in the family bonds of love, and so I have given several examples. The mothers may be in no danger of dying, although some are, and yet believe they have died.

Birth is a moment when the woman's link with the material, logical world is at its weakest. Whether you believe that a child comes to this world from another more spiritual dimension, 'trailing clouds of glory' as Wordsworth put it, or whether it is viewed simply as the child's passage from the intra-uterine world to the mother's arms, the baby's moment of entry is one of intense physical, emotional, psychological and perhaps psychic energy.

As with near-death experiences, these near-birth experiences may be wonderful and give the woman a new insight into life. Or they can be absolutely terrifying. They occur mainly during difficult or painful births.

Tanya's near-birth experience linked not only with her unborn daughter, but with her own mother, and was ultimately a link with all mothers and the spirit of motherhood:

'I had my third child in a nursing home 22 years ago. I was in labour when I got to the home at 11.30 at night. The midwife would not believe me and refused to examine me. She insisted I had a sleeping pill. I refused. My husband was there. She said, "Stop being a nuisance", and added that if I was in labour the pill would make absolutely no difference.

"If not, we'll all be able to get some sleep," she said. So, reluctantly, I took the pill.

'My waters broke suddenly and the midwife started to panic. My doctor had promised to be with me, but the midwife refused to call him. Even my husband was not allowed to stay. After five hours of very bad pain, I asked for something to relieve it. The midwife refused.

"Why not?" I was exhausted.

"You had a sleeping pill," she replied. "You are on your own."

'I realised I was in trouble. I went very light-headed. A feeling of dying came over me. I became calm as I realised I was dying.

'I very nearly drowned as a child. Now I had the same sensation. At this point, a voice in my head cut across my thoughts. "You must ask for help."

'I started to argue. "I have already asked for help, but she won't give me any."

"Ask the mother for help."

"She did not help me when I asked her anyway."

'My father, who was a doctor, had been at my birth. He told me that during labour my mother cried out for her own mother in her pain, and my father had been very contemptuous of what he saw as her weakness.

'When the voice said, "Ask the mother for help," I had not wanted to ask for my mother as she had done at my birth, because my father had told me such behaviour was silly and childish. Now I had a blinding realisation whom I must ask for help.

'I said aloud, "I am not a believer," and resisted. Eventually, I cried out, "Mama Mia, help me." But the racking pain continued, and I waited at the end of the contraction for peace. Another contraction started straight away.

'I was angry. I had done what I was asked to do and had been convinced help would come. At the peak of the pain, it stopped. One moment, it was so intense, knife-like, then instantly it cut out.

"Thank God, thank God," I cried out in overwhelming gratitude, over and over again.

'My eyes were closed. I heard the midwife say, "Tanya, move your leg. Come on, move your leg. We have to get the baby".

"I have moved my leg," I replied.

'There was a slapping sound, but I could not feel anything. "I think we have lost her," the midwife called out to someone

I could not see.

"No, I'm fine," I answered, and I was. I opened my eyes and could not understand what was happening. Someone had lowered the ceiling to a couple of feet above my face. I looked towards my feet. There was a light on a wire. I was disorientated. I looked round and was looking down on to the heads of the midwife. Another nurse wheeled in a huge cream machine. There was a parting in the midwife's hair. She had dyed hair, and I could see the different colour of her hair growing through. To the left was a hospital screen near where I was lying. I could see over the top, and a nurse ran behind the screen and was frantically dialling from the phone that was attached to the wall. I discovered later the phone was not visible from my bed. Then I tried to work out what was happening. I asked myself, "Have I got a body, have I got a leg to move?"

'I was convinced I had, as I could sense the outline of my body, just as you can when you shut your eyes when you are awake.

'I could hear, I could see, I could talk, but no one could hear me, I realised.

'I was absolutely at peace, altogether, complete. That "me" was, however, no longer attached to my body. Then I heard a voice, the same firm, male voice who had told me I must ask for help, telling me "You must go back. You must go back," it repeated.

"No, I am not going back," I answered.

'Then the voice said, "What about your baby?"

'I had totally forgotten.

'Then I was reminded of my other two children. "Yes, of course, I have two other children and a husband".

'I had another life. I agreed. "Yes, I suppose I have to go back."

'As soon as the thought formed, everything went black. I was conscious of a heaviness like weights, like sacks of flour all over me. It was very unclear. The midwife was saying. "Thank goodness, she's coming round."

'In a different tone, she spoke to me, "Now, Tanya, try and move your leg." I tried, but it was like a ton of bricks.

"Now push." The baby was born. Apparently I had

haemorrhaged before the baby was born, and had lost a pint and a half of blood. The placenta had ripped before delivery.

'My experience changed my life. I had no idea until then I had a soul or spirit. I was left with a tremendous yearning and motivation to do something worthwhile with my life. I eventually did a theology degree, though I had three kids at the time. I also later took a course in counselling. I felt in need of counselling myself. I vowed to talk about my vision and use it for the benefit of others.'

Unlike Tanya, for Bess the experience began after the baby was born, when her life was not in danger and she was not under the influence of analgesics:

'I was only 20 when I gave birth to my first child. I found myself feeling very lonely and frightened during labour, which was excruciatingly painful. I remember praying to God for the pain to end, and to die.

'I had a daughter, and was placed in a three-bedded room of which I was the only occupant. I dropped off into an uneasy sleep and awoke to find my nose one or two inches from the ceiling. I looked down on myself and thought I was looking at my twin sister. I realised it was me.

'I felt frightened momentarily, but found myself drifting peacefully and naturally down a dark tunnel with a bright light at the end. This seemed to happen very quickly. I arrived at the end, and a person on the other side spoke to me. I could hear a voice but not see any form, as the light was so bright. The voice knew who I was, and seemed kind and loving.

'He asked me, "Who would look after the baby if you died?" We went through the possibilities, and I said I agreed, I would have to go back to care for my daughter. Instantly, I was back in my body and in pain.'

The call of the new-born infant is a major factor in the mother's decision to return to this world, as is the need to care for other children. Although the experience may last only minutes or even seconds, its effect is more long reaching. It can even have an important effect on the bonding process. Jennifer, who almost died during childbirth, is convinced that her baby shared her experience:

'I was nine months pregnant and started to bleed heavily.

The doctor put an oxygen mask over my face. Next I was in a dark, dark, tunnel which branched in two. I was travelling down the dark tunnel to the junction. I had to choose which road to take. One was jagged and bumpy and very dark. The other was smooth as silk, a pure cylinder with white light at the end.

'Every ounce of power that was in me pulled me towards the easy route. I screamed inside at the thought of the jagged one. Suddenly an unbelievable surge of strength, which can only be described as a dam breaking, forced me down a terrible, endless, dark, jagged, tunnel, down and down. There was no escape. A voice echoed over and over in my head, "Who cares anyway? Who cares anyway? Who cares?"

'I floated up to the ceiling and watched the nurse tell me I had a baby boy. I could see the clock on the wall. I watched myself smile, but it was not me. I floated down again. When I woke up the doctor told me I was lucky to be alive. He called my son a miracle baby. He had nearly died too.

'Sadly, I did not feel any bond with my baby. My husband says when the baby was born, he screamed and screamed. He had never heard a baby cry like that before. I feel certain the baby had a similar experience and that he, too, would have gone down the smooth artery if that force had not pulled us both. I suppose I will never know.

'Recently, however, my son fell downstairs, and for a few seconds he hugged me tenderly and I hugged him.'

Jennifer is at last bonding with her son. Where there are problems as a result of an NBE, it may be because the woman is not able to talk it through without disbelief and even suspicion by some professionals.

However, for Paula the NBE, which occurred a short time after the birth, actually awakened her bond with her infant:

'My experience happened two days after the birth of my son. It was not a pleasant labour, and for some reason after my baby was born I did not immediately love him. I was shocked because when my daughter had been born, I had experienced an overwhelming love for her, yet I didn't for my son. It was all I could do to feed him. I was ashamed of myself. Two days after he was born, I was lying in bed and I did not feel too well, though it was nothing serious.

'I was in the middle bed of a three-bed ward. We settled down for the night. To my amazement, I floated up to the ceiling. It was dark and I felt very alone. I turned my head to look down and I could see myself clearly, as I lay face upwards on the bed. I kept floating at no particular speed. I thought I might have died and remember calling out that I loved my son and wanted to go back to look after him. Now I did want to hold and cuddle him and to see my daughter again. Because I didn't want my children to have no mother, I was desperate to return, and kept asking to return over and over again. The next thing I remember was being back in my body and the nurse coming in and switching on the light, saying she heard someone calling for help. Afterwards, I was able to bond with my son.'

The pressure on women to feel an instant, overwhelming love for their child is immense, and a mother can feel very guilty when this does not happen.

Diane's experience is slightly different, as it occurred during a Caesarean operation. I have had four Caesareans and have had no such experiences, although I have heard of similar visions to Diane's, one from a woman who was awake for part of the operation, but unable to tell anyone. The story Diane tells is intriguing as it is deeply embedded in her relationships, and also because she feels it gave her an especially deep bond with her son. Diane knew she was having a boy, although she gave birth before ultra-scans were used. Many women do know the sex of an unborn child from the moment of conception:

'I had to have an emergency Caesarean. I was given no pre-medication. I found myself in total blackness. I said, "Where are the stars?" At that moment, I was aware of a beautiful male voice, reassuring me. "You must not worry about this. It is just one of life's lessons we must learn."

'I saw my husband in the darkness. Another man was present, Colin, a dear friend who had helped me many times when I was alone or worried. The voice told me "Colin will always be there for you and he will devote his life to you. You have a son."

'I came round in agony and could not speak, and yet I was

in total bliss because of my experience. Everyone I met looked like angels, and I could see into their souls. My son was badly jaundiced and in intensive care for a while, yet in spite of the anxiety and pain, my body was in complete joy and harmony.

'My marriage did break up but, as the voice had told me, Colin was there for me and helped me through my troubles.'

Diane's bond with her son has remained very strong: 'My son Tom had a bad attack of epilepsy when he was born. However, the problem was under control and he had not had an attack for years. After my husband and I had separated, my son sometimes used to stay with his father. One morning, as I was driving Tom, who was by now 15, to the station for a visit, I had an ache in my chest and a growing unease that something would go seriously wrong.

During the day I had the strongest desire to ring my husband's home, although I did not normally check up. I did not have my address book with me, as I was away in London. With difficulty, I resisted the urge to dial Directory Enquiries, although the anxiety was growing. I did not want to seem a fussy mother. As soon as I reached home at 10.30 p.m. I gave in to the mounting panic and rang my husband. My son was in hospital. He had had a seizure.'

Near-death visions are sometimes seen as glimpses of the world that waits beyond. Many people are reassured by them that death is not the end, and that as we do pass into the unknown our loved ones will be waiting, as at the beginning of our life.

# 13

# MOVING CLOSER

At the point of death and immediately afterwards, the two worlds seem to move closer. Many dying people claim to see already deceased relatives coming to greet them, and even offer comfort to grieving relatives at their own funeral.

Pauline told me how she witnessed her father's death-bed vision:

'My dad had a stroke before he died and could not speak properly. One night he sat up and said quite clearly, "Mum's come for me."

'My mother had been dead for some years, and I reminded Dad gently she was no longer with us. However, he insisted, "No, your mother has been here, and she says she'll come back later and take me for a walk."

'Dad died at 2 a.m. with a smile on his face.'

May was in her fifties when she died, and like my own mother, was ravaged by the effects of her long illness. I met her son Andrew at a book signing in Exeter. May was in hospital, and the night she died Andrew was sitting next to her holding her hand. Suddenly May sat up, smiled, and Andrew told me, looked as though there was a rainbow behind her head. Andrew realised his mother was looking beyond him towards the door: "Gran," she said, "yes, I'm just a bit tired. Take me home, Gran. I can smell the lilies".

Andrew's mother reached out and her face became young, like a young girl's, the face he had seen in the photographs of her as a young girl when she had lived with her grandmother. May had told him many times that her granny's home always smelled of lilies. Moments later May died.

Andrew saw what he described as a rainbow around his mother's head, which some people believe is an aura. Many experiences at the point of, or just after death, seem to involve lights. One theory is that the brightness is the ethereal body leaving the earthly one. Others see light as a way the dead and dying may communicate without frightening us. Pearl believes her uncle chose to contact her in this way so that she would not be afraid:

'My uncle lived a sad life. He was blind, and died at Christmas, when he was only 48. I was very upset by my uncle's death. He had always said he would come back and let us know if there was anything after death. However, I hated the idea of ghosts and would have been terrified to have seen him, though I wanted to know he was all right.

'The night before his cremation, I was reading in bed and feeling so sorry about the waste of my uncle's life. Suddenly I looked up. The door was closed. In front of the door were the most beautiful lights that stayed for several minutes. I knew it was my uncle, and that he was happy at last.'

Those of us who have been touched by a death in the family know that it is impossible for life ever to be the same again. While some relations do share death-bed visions and see their loved ones well and happy after death, for many the experience is more subtle, although no less spiritual and meaningful.

Marian and I were friends at college. Although we have not seen each other for some years, we correspond every Christmas. Recently Marian's mother, who was very kind to me after my own mother's death, herself died after a difficult illness. Marian described the last months of her mother's life in a letter I will always treasure. I include the story in this book because it may be that all we can do for our dying loved ones is to take them to the brink of the other side. Once they are gone, we can only wait for a sign that they are still with us.

Marian's story, about an ordinary, busy family facing death with courage and humour, may help many people facing similar tragedies, and explains better than I can the enduring and all-powerful nature of family bonds:

'At the beginning of the end, Mom saw the four of us, myself, my dad and my brother Malcolm, as a magic circle. If we all held on tight, we'd beat death, and we tried. We were in turns ecstatic when something good happened, distraught when the tables turned. We laughed and joked endlessly – but then we always have.

'When we brought Mom home for the last time, I pushed Malcolm in a wheelchair to the ward. Dad followed, scolding, with a jar of sweets for the staff. A bit of a bump and my brother was propelled from the chair like a jack-in-the-box. We were laughing and silly, overjoyed to be taking my mother home. Although we knew we had so little time, all we could see was that we were taking our mom where she belonged.

'We never left her. She wanted Dad with her 24 hours a day and he was, no grumbles.

'At the end, Mom was so afraid. She hated being anywhere on her own and though we were with her, holding her hands as she slipped away, I knew she was alone. I got so far. It was dark and I was so afraid. There were shadows and whisperings, but I could not see past that. I didn't have the words then, and I don't now.

'The funeral was sparkling, a shining sort of day, bright sun, masses of colours in the flowers, and monumental figures in black, in shiny black cars with gleaming chrome.

'We arrived at the church, Dad and I. My brother, husband and two cousins were to bear the coffin. No one else was going to carry our mom. At the end of a tunnel of trees, the vicar appeared and drew us into the day. We followed the coffin up to the old lych-gate, which was shoulder high. Four six-footers and a lot of flowers was too high.

"Bend the knees a little, gentlemen, please."

'Bearing solid oak with mahogany veneers and lots of brass – nothing too good for our mother – the coffin bearers faltered. Suddenly it was as if she was there. That bubble of mirth rose inside as I caught her eye, and we homed in together on four pairs of strapping knees trembling in unison as they limboed under that gate. I wanted to laugh but, of course, I didn't. The vicar finished the service by saying, "She was such a lovely lady", and truly she was'.

Like Marian's mother, Angela's mum wanted to go home to die. Angela went to hospital to see her mother, who was so ill she could not talk. One morning, however, her mother was totally lucid and said, "Why are you crying?"

Angela was amazed. "Because I'm upset about you," she replied.

"I'll be all right".

Then Angela's mother asked "Home?"

"My home?" Angela asked and her mother nodded. Home was the last word she ever spoke:

'I took her home, nursed her and she died peacefully. There was a sweet fragrance around Mum during those last few weeks of her illness, and my daughter said several times after her death, "Nan's here". At such moments, we could smell again that sweet scent of those last days'.

Finally, love may sometimes enable us to push back the barriers of death and make the last days full of love and laughter. Professor George Wall, Professor of Philosophy at the University of Lamar in Texas, told me, when I met him in Oxford, how the close bond of love between himself and his wife enabled her to return from a living death to say goodbye and share a few more weeks of deep communication together:

'My wife knew she was dying. She became incoherent at Christmas 1986. We both desperately wanted to say goodbye but we could not do it, as we could not communicate directly. Amelia was distraught about dying. One evening, Amelia was really sick. I put her to bed. She rested, and when I went to see her about 10.15 p.m. the difference was truly amazing.

'I knew something had happened. Though Amelia was wasting away, now she looked radiant. The beauty shone from her.

"Amelia," I asked, "what has happened?"

'My wife was perfectly coherent, although three hours before, she was totally incoherent.

"Oh George, I've been to God".

"What happened, were you praying?", though I knew in her state it was impossible.

"I don't know. It is indescribable. I saw an eastern-style figure by a river, and I knew I had to go with the flow and not fight".

'Amelia was elated, on a spiritual high. I called our friends and they danced round the room with joy at the miracle. It was as if she had been sent back into reality. She remained coherent for six weeks. Amelia was never happy about dying, but she told me on the evening of her awakening, "I still have a fear of death, George, but the anger has been taken away. I want to remain here with you and the girls and our friends, but I know I won't be alone."

'A week before the experience I was swimming at the YMCA when I felt I had to pray, not for her healing but her peace. Amelia remained coherent until a month before her death. We had those precious extra days to be together and say goodbye.'

A family that communicates on the deepest spiritual level, and for whom no subject is taboo or subject to mockery, enables its members to move away physically without guilt, knowing that the link of love is still there in times of crisis and loneliness. If we can encourage mutual intuitive links and use family psychic experiences to enrich family life, then we can move from the consumer and achievement-oriented society that offers no real happiness or permanence. Whether the family is a two-some, includes children and older members, or is a glorious mix of foster, step or adopted links and parents, close intuitive bonds can make relationships. This can be fulfilling. This wordless communication can operate on a spiritual level and provide an underlying assurance of love and acceptance, even if everyday problems cause strife.

I do not believe that children should be introduced to formal psychic practices, and whatever age the family, ouija board sessions and seances can be dangerous, whether on a psychic or psychological level. Nor should the psychic become more important than the everyday world. We should not let the dead or living dictate our destinies, and no truly loving relation would want to. However, as part of family life, an intuitive approach can be enriching and give us access to knowledge, not available to logic. Spontaneous paranormal experiences, whether everyday telepathy or more dramatic occurrences, need no deliberate development or formal exercises.

However, it is possible and I believe, desirable, to provide an atmosphere and way of life where natural intuitive bonds can flourish. In such a setting, there is time and peace to listen to the inner promptings of joint family wisdom. In many homes such gentle support and acceptance are automatic. However, in modern society we are pressurised by images of the perfect family, attained by buying the right products and relying on outward symbols of success and happiness. There is also the totally false expectation that we have an automatic right to happiness, and if sorrow or misfortune strike, we or those closest to us, are somehow to blame.

At the end of this book I offer suggestions to encourage intuition and bonds that offers security, not suffocation, that have worked with my own family and people I know.

If you are alone, not from choice but circumstance, or have only unhappy family memories, this book may seem alien and irrelevant. Families aren't ideal or proof against unhappiness or loss. Even if you cannot or do not want to be with your own kin, there may be another human being with whom you can relate through friendship. Many children today don't have everyday contact with grandparents, who may live far away. They may welcome the input of an older person in their lives. Friends and workmates, too, can become very dear, and give us the close acceptance we need.

All families change and we can all experience life on a deeper, more spiritual level, by reaching out to others, even if they are not our blood relations or love partner. Life makes no promises of for ever or eternal happiness, and sometimes we can't understand how life can be so cruel and unfair. Real relationships can be dull or even unhappy for long periods, and yet survive and grow stronger. If we can find love and acceptance with those for whom we care, though sometimes find irritating beyond belief, then life can have some joy and consolation.

Success with no one to rejoice with us, can be hollow. It is one of my deepest regrets that my own parents, who suffered many hardships and disappointments, can't see my books in print. My own mother sent a story every week to the *Birmingham Mail*, and each week received a polite rejection slip. I don't think that newspaper even published fiction. Maybe my family do know, and my mum is saying, "All kippers and curtains and up to her ears in H.P". My dad will be warning me not to get above myself. As for my Aunty Ruth, she will still be asking, as she did in life, why I don't write proper books like Barbara Cartland?

The family is the beginning of the journey we all make through life. Sometimes it is good, sometimes mediocre and occasionally frankly awful. As we get older we can understand the mistakes of our parents, if not forgive them. And however far we move physically and emotionally from a family, there is still a bond.

Sceptics tell us that all these links are explained through conditioning. Visions of beloved grannie or loving relatives, waiting for us when we die are, they assure us, hallucinations caused by dying brain cells. Scientists do not know, and will not perhaps realise, until they see their mum or dad calling them, that all the logic and theories in the world are no substitute for homely comfort.

We may never have a life and death premonition concerning our loved ones, but on an everyday level we can, as the accounts in this book tell, link into their love and support. As I end the book amid the chaos of my crowded front room, where I write and the children watch their videos and crunch crisps into the carpet, psychic links seem a million miles away. All families are, however, at root psychic and spiritual; some use these channels more easily than others. So trust your instincts, not to transform your family into those whiter than white ever-smiling creatures of the adverts, but to make each day a little special.

# 14

# FIFTEEN WAYS OF ENCOURAGING POSITIVE PSYCHIC FAMILY BONDS

1. Keep a psychic family book, just like any other family record, containing family legends and everyday examples of telepathy and prediction. We always think we will remember these incidents, but the details can get hazy over the years. A book with any legends, family superstitions and natural cures for illness that have been in the family since time immemorial, is a wonderful record that can be handed down from generation to generation.

   You might like to keep a section for baby experiences, whether it is your baby, that of a brother or sister, or an expected grandchild. There is nothing unlucky about starting notes from the moment of conception. Write down any inklings of sex or what the baby will be like. We often dream of unborn children, but forget the details so quickly. It's not only the mother-to-be who dreams about a new baby, but other close family members.

   If you have an infant, note when you woke before the baby, the times you knew the baby was in distress, or your young child picked up your thoughts. Grandparents often have strong links with grandchildren, who are adept at reading their minds.

2.  Trust your instincts concerning your family, whatever age
    they may be. If you feel concerned about a family mem-
    ber, make tactful enquiries. Save such intervention for
    those times when you feel instinctively, rather than
    logically, that there is something wrong.

    Try to gauge intuitively underlying moods before any
    family confrontations. The issue under fire may be a
    smoke-screen for the real worry or fear.

    If you suddenly link into an absent family member,
    phone or write simply to say, "I love you" or "I was think-
    ing of you." They may well need a boost, or may just be
    feeling unloved. This is not the same as constantly inter-
    fering in the lives of our family. Indeed, possessive peo-
    ple tend to be the least psychically aware.

3.  Protect your family against hostile vibes from the outside
    world or the fears conjured up by anxieties within. Crys-
    tals, such as rose quartz, amethyst or smoked grey quartz,
    can help to absorb negative influences. Use a clear piece
    of crystal quartz, which need not be very expensive, to
    replace the negative with positive.

    Children can be afraid of the dark or nameless phan-
    toms that nevertheless seem very real to them. Enclosing
    the child in an invisible pink pyramid or soft purple cloud
    can be reassuring.

    If a family member is under external threat or having
    problems at work or school, you can protect him/her with
    the power of your love, like the Canadian squaw in the
    legend, who saved her son from the eagle. You maybe
    can't sock your partner's haranguing boss in the jaw or
    physically set about the bullies who tease your child,
    tempting though it is. You can, however, cast around the
    threatened person a psychic cloak of invisibility. Jasper
    stones are very good for this, as is jet.

    Send especially loving thoughts and perhaps light as
    you blow out a candle, to family members who may be
    feeling alienated from the family group.

4.  Make a specific time, if only once a week, when all family
    members, wherever they are, link in thought, if only for a

few moments. It's a reminder you are not alone, and a few extra positive vibes in the universe can't be bad. Teenagers may laugh at the idea, but in times of stress, they like to know that the boring but reassuring protection of the family unit is there.

If you are away from young children, let them know you regularly send them messages of love, and that they can do the same. This is very different from trying to enter a relation or partner's mind to manipulate their thought or influence their actions. Sometimes I'll see one of the younger three's faces come into my mind, and I always say 'Hello'.

5.  Spend time being together, rather than dashing from one activity to another, whether you are a two-some or a four-generation extended family. It is easy to be pressurised to join countless activities in our leisure time and shunt our children from one learning experience to another, and end up feeling exhausted and fractious.

    Listen to and value the stories of the older generation, for such tales are part of family folklore. The modern emphasis is on youth, but the insights of the older generation can root the family in a sure foundation and put present problems into perspective.

    It is in the silences, the quiet moments, whether on a walk or just sitting without conversation that the intuition flows. This can provide a space for younger family members to voice worries, hopes and fears.

6.  Do not force a child to independence from home before he or she is ready. Some children aren't joiners, and even the friendliest playgroup may seem daunting unless the child is ready to move away.

7.  Encourage family members to discuss all kinds of experiences. As a society we tend to find it easier to talk about sex, drugs and alcohol problems rather than psychic issues. An older person who talks to a dead partner may be secretly afraid he or she is going mad. Someone who is ill or is just getting on in years may want

to discuss death and the after-life.

"Oh, you've got years left yet" is perhaps more helpful in shielding our own fears at losing someone we love, than allaying those of a grandparent who might want to bring the issue of dying into the open.

Children need to talk within a secure family environment about death, especially when they hear of a child dying. Pet deaths are a good way of approaching the subject. My own children always call plane trails, "Tiger (a favourite hamster) going for a walk in the sky".

8.  Accept dreams and visions, not as prophecies of doom, but as a clue to the inner dynamics of the family. Family members may have similar dreams and these can give a clue, not only to underlying dilemmas but to possible solutions. If you do have a vivid warning dream concerning your family – very different from a nightmare or natural anxiety – listen to it. At the worst you'll look a fool.

9.  Encourage simple family rituals, whether you are a twosome or have six children. For children, candle birthday wishes, stones and crystals are natural ways of tuning into the rhythms of the elements. Children have no inhibitions with stones and crystals, picking those instinctively that will cure a headache or drive away nightmares.

    Get up to watch the sunrise and sunset on the shortest and longest days, visit old stone circles and walk in the wind and rain, or watch the tide turning.

10. Cut down on second-hand living – television, videos, computer games. When we are tired and busy, it's easier to eat in front of the television or hire a video for the kids while you sort things out. I am as guilty as the next parent or I would never have got this book written. A simple, communally prepared shared meal even once a week, a Sunday morning walk or even a quiet ten minutes last thing at night, can centre the family and encourage positive connections. The old, maligned night-time 'slippers and cocoa' routine served a basic human need.

11. Concentrate on priorities in family life, and remember that time is finite. If it is a lovely day, go out together if possible. Equally if a partner, parent or child is sad or worried, leave non-essentials and make time to listen or just be around to be ignored. Enjoy each day in some way. Even if a particular family member is being difficult, try to see something positive in the relationship. The old maxim, 'Do not let the sun go down on your anger', has more than a grain of truth in it.

12. Value the unique qualities of family members, including yourself, and don't equate conformity with true together-ness. Families who never argue may find it hard to display warmth. Siblings who claim to feel no rivalry may feel deep guilt and resentment in later years.

    Children can easily feel diminished when their wrong-doings are regarded as a sign of worthlessness. Equally, it is hurtful at any age to be compared unfavourably with those who may seem more successful in the world's eyes. Many adults carry the scars of early criticism by those closest to them.

13. However, occasionally a family member may bear the seeds of his/her own destruction. A critical mother who manipulates adult children to compete for her favours, a father who cannot allow children to grow up, a parent who favours one child to the exclusion of any others, or a critical partner, may be unhappy rather than deliberately malicious. Love, accompanied by a refusal to be emo-tionally blackmailed, may overcome the carping, that itself can have been caused in the past by an over-critical, older family member. However, if wounds cannot be healed we can only walk away rather than be destroyed. No human being has the right to the soul of another, and the strong bond of family love, if twisted, can be lethal.

14. Remember to include new family members in the psychic and emotional life of the family, whether step-children, in-laws or a new partner after a divorce. The everyday

sphere may be fraught with the pitfalls of changing faces and conflicting loyalties. If you can communicate acceptance on a deeper level, then the us/them divide can, with time and goodwill, be breached. A family that is unable to adapt and move forward can become stagnant and keep its members from growing.

15. Finally, don't try too hard to be perfect whether parent, grandparent, child or partner. Anxiety, guilt and unrealistic expectations can actually block intuitive links and insights. I was so uptight trying to be a good mother and wife when my first two children were young, I blocked those vital channels.

     We all yell, say awful things and wish we were single, orphans, childless or part of one of the gleaming, smiling families on the television adverts. If the underlying love is there, that is enough to sustain the family through good times and bad.

*If you have enjoyed this book you will enjoy:*

# Psychic Power of Children

Cassandra Eason's study of the paranormal abilities of ordinary children began after her two-and-a-half-year-old son 'saw' his father having a motor-cycle accident 40 miles away. After talking to other mothers, she realised that such incidents were neither uncommon nor anything to be afraid of.

The book, re-issued by Foulsham, with many new cases, looks at telepathy, predicition, invisible friends and phantom foes, and the ghosts of children. It deals with a delicate subject in a sensitive manner which is also down-to-earth and humorous.

# Psychic Suburbia

Is it true that ghosts prefer ruined castles or lonely moors? No, they don't.

Popular psychic communicator and broadcaster Cassandra Eason receives countless letters and regular phone-in reports of everyday hauntings and other paranormal phenomena – all in conventional terraces and 'semis' that look anything but ghostly.

This book relates dozens of cases, from poltergeists and premonitions to near-death experiences and astral projection, showing how ordinary people in ordinary places can attract extraordinary signals from the spirit world.

Read about the Huddersfield seance at which the *Marchioness* riverboat disaster was vividly experienced while it happened in London. Accompany one of the subjects on an out-of-body tour of a Berkshire town, and check out more than one instance of psychic promptings that have averted death on the motorway.

*Cassandra Eason is also the author of the:*

# Today's Woman Divination series

Each is written in the same easy-to-follow style and, in a six-week course, concentrates on developing your powers of intuition rather than relying on expensive clairvoyants to choose your path for you.

Once you have learned one system, it is very easy to move on to the other forms of divination described in these books.

# Rune Divination
# for Today's Woman

Many women don't use the runes for divination because, at first sight, they seem so complicated. But you do not have to be a Viking or professor of Old Norse to tap your own hidden powers.

Step by step, this book shows you how, by drawing simple symbols on pebbles, you can tap into a magic that is as fresh today as when Nordic and Anglo-Saxon women first tried to juggle relationships and family with the need for finding their own identities.

# Pendulum Divination
# for Today's Woman

Whether your pendulum is finest crystal or an old key on a piece of string, you can use it to dowse, not for oil or water, but for your future options and your present health. The system uses simple circle cloths to focus your natural intuitive wisdom and ensure that you stay in control of your own decision-making.

There are also sections on finding lost objects, dowsing for health and even – for the more adventurous – dowsing for ghosts.

# Tarot Divination for Today's Woman

At first sight, the ancient symbols of the Tarot cards appear to have nothing to do with modern life. But they can easily be adapted to the lives of women today, using a very simple spread to build up a picture of the options which life is making available to you.

For this is fortune-making, not fortune-telling and relies, not on some external magic, but on your own very powerful intuitions.

# Crystal Divination for Today's Woman

Crystals and semi-precious stones provide a very powerful form of divination by harnessing the energies of your own powerful inner magic.

You don't need to be the fabulously wealthy owner of a vast collection of gems, nor an expert geologist, to use the system. It is a simple – and cheap – system which is based on a very simple colour method which you can adapt to your own special needs.

# I Ching Divination for Today's Woman

Take away the image of the male Chinese civil servant which until now has dominated the I Ching and it reflects a woman's natural approach to magic and change. Using the more ancient system, based on the natural forces of fire, sky, water, earth, trees, thunder, mountains and lakes, women can interpret their own present and plan the future. The book shows how to make simple I Ching pebbles to work out your trigrams in seconds.

# Moon Divination for Today's Woman

Moon divination puts women in touch with their natural inner cycles that, from the beginning of time, have been linked with the phases of the moon. It uses planet stones made from ordinary materials and a moon cloth to harness the power of our inner astrology. But the book is not about worshipping a moon goddess. It deals with the everyday problems of a modern woman.

# *About the Author*

Cassandra Eason is a mother of five children and lives on the Isle of Wight. She juggles writing and broadcasting with taking care of the family, and the vacuum cleaner with the word processor, and frequently ends up fusing both. From an ordinary home in the back streets of Birmingham, she won a scholarship to an exclusive school (her Dad's bike would be parked alongside the Rolls-Royces at open evenings).

She became a teacher and then married a nice middle-class boy, but found out that nice china at tea-time wasn't the same as a warm heart. They split up and Cassandra was rescued from a tumbledown cottage in Cornwall, with two small children, by a middle-aged knight in a Renault 4, whom she later married. Together they had three more children.

While the children were small, Cassandra took a degree in psychology with the idea of returning to teaching once the youngsters took up a little less of her time. But she was pushed into a writing career when her middle son, Jack, told her casually over breakfast that his Dad was falling off his motor bike as it was happening 40 miles away.

The response from ordinary mothers to whom she related this experience led to her first book, *The Psychic Power of Children,* which looks at the extra-ordinary psychic experiences of ordinary people, rather than concentrating on the tales of famous haunted castles and the phantoms of the gentry. This book has now been re-published, in a revised version with many new cases, by Foulsham.

Cassandra's interest in divination methods, such as the Tarot and the runes, began while she was researching *The Psychic Power of Children* and *Psychic Suburbia.*

Since the publication of the *Today's Woman* series, she has appeared on radio and television, demon-strating her methods of fortune-making rather than fortune-telling.

Cassandra is always pleased to hear from readers about their experiences and tries to answer all letters. She can be contacted through her publisher.